THE
ACCOUNT OF THE
TABERNACLE

TRANSLATION AND
TEXTUAL PROBLEMS OF THE
GREEK EXODUS

BY

D. W. GOODING

M.A., Ph.D.

*Sometime Major Open Scholar and Senior Scholar of
Trinity College, Cambridge
Research Fellow of the Durham Colleges in
the University of Durham*

CAMBRIDGE
AT THE UNIVERSITY PRESS
1959

PUBLISHED BY

THE SYNDICS OF THE CAMBRIDGE UNIVERSITY PRESS

Bentley House, 200 Euston Road, London, N.W. 1
American Branch: 32 East 57th Street, New York 22, N.Y.

©

CAMBRIDGE UNIVERSITY PRESS

1959

Printed in Great Britain at the University Press, Cambridge
(Brooke Crutchley, University Printer)

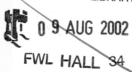

TEXTS AND STUDIES

CONTRIBUTIONS TO
BIBLICAL AND PATRISTIC LITERATURE

NEW SERIES

Edited by
C. H. DODD

VI

THE ACCOUNT OF THE
TABERNACLE

IN THIS SERIES

PATRI MEO

QUO DUCE

SACRAS LITTERAS

AB INFANTIA NOVI DILEXIQUE

HOC OPUSCULUM

GRATO PIOQUE ANIMO

DEDICO

CONTENTS

PREFACE

This book is a by-product of stricter studies in the textual criticism of the Greek Pentateuch, and that explains in part why it approaches the problem it discusses almost entirely from the point of view of the Septuagint evidence. It does not thereby deny or forget the importance of other lines of approach. On the other hand the Septuagint is both a main factor in the problem and one of the chief sources of evidence for its solution. It seemed a sound procedure therefore to make a separate examination of the Septuagint evidence so that its bearing on the wider problem could be more clearly perceived.

It is no longer an idle hope that one day a further discovery of ancient Hebrew manuscripts will provide evidence that will settle the textual problems of the end of Exodus conclusively. Already Qumrān has produced a fragment of the earlier chapters of Exodus, while its longer portions from the historical books have shed much welcome light on the various Hebrew text traditions that lie behind that part of the Septuagint. Meanwhile we cannot afford to sit still, even though many of our present conclusions may later need to be revised.

The helpful article by the Rev. A. H. Finn (*J.T.S.* vol. xvi, pp. 449–82) on this same problem did not come to my notice until my own work was almost complete. For that reason references to his work are in my earlier chapters confined almost entirely to the footnotes. While we share many general conclusions, his work is both wider and narrower in scope than mine: wider in that he deals with the source-problems of the Hebrew text, and narrower in that he does not undertake so detailed an examination of the Greek. Moreover it appears that he was unaware of Julius Popper's book, which contains perhaps the strongest and most detailed work of any on this problem. Finn has, in consequence, no answers to Popper's special arguments.

In view of the difference of verse-numbering between the Greek and the Hebrew I have given wherever necessary both the Greek and Hebrew references. Where editions of the Greek text differ between them in the verse-numbering I have adhered consistently to the system used by Brooke–McLean, for the simple reason that their rich storehouse has been my constant source of information. Readers using other editions will occasionally notice discrepancies, but they will not, I think, be inconvenienced thereby, and I have on that account refrained from cumbering my text with alternative Greek references.

It is a pleasure to acknowledge the help received from Mr H. Allen, Mr J. D. Hartburn, Mr E. A. Rose, Mr Andrew Walls, Professor J. Ziegler of Würzburg University and the Rev. Dr W. P. M. Walters (Peter Katz), all of whom read through my manuscript at one stage or another and made valuable criticisms and suggestions. To Dr Walters my debt is immeasurably large. It was under his guidance that I first embarked on Septuagint studies, and to his constant help and encouragement I owe more than I can express.

My thanks are due also to the Durham Colleges and to Dr J. Conway Davies in particular for the shelter and encouragement they have given to these studies. I am gratefully conscious too of the honour Professor C. H. Dodd has conferred on the work by receiving it into the noble company of Texts and Studies. Finally, the readers and printers of the University Press deserve high praise for their excellent workmanship.

D. W. G.

Durham

September 1958

LIST OF MAIN REFERENCES

ADDIS, W. E. *The Documents of the Hexateuch*, vol. II. London, 1898.
BROOKE–MCLEAN. *The Old Testament in Greek*, ed. by A. E. Brooke and N. McLean. Cambridge, 1906– .
FIELD, F. *Origenis Hexaplorum Quae Supersunt*. Oxford, Clarendon Press, 1875.
FINN, A. H. 'The Tabernacle Chapters', *Journal of Theological Studies*, vol. XVI, pp. 449–82, July 1915.
HATCH–REDPATH. *A Concordance to the Septuagint*, by E. Hatch and H. A. Redpath. Oxford, 1897.
KATZ, PETER. *Philo's Bible*. Cambridge, 1950.
KENNEDY, H. A. A. Article on the Tabernacle in Hasting's *Dictionary of the Bible*, vol. IV.
LIDDELL and SCOTT. *A Greek–English Lexicon*, new edition by H. Stuart Jones and R. McKenzie. Oxford.
MCNEILE, A. H. *The Book of Exodus*. Westminster Commentaries, London, 1908.
MOFFATT, JAMES. *The Old Testament, A New Translation*, vol. I. London, 1924.
POPPER, JULIUS. *Der biblische Bericht über die Stiftshütte*. Leipzig, 1862.
RAHLFS, A. *Septuaginta*. Stuttgart, 1935.
SCHLEUSNER. *Novus Thesaurus philologico-criticus sive Lexicon in LXX*, ed. J. Fr. Schleusner. London, 1829.
SMITH, W. ROBERTSON. *The Old Testament in the Jewish Church*, 2nd ed. London and Edinburgh, 1892.
SWETE, H. B. *Introduction to the Old Testament in Greek*. Cambridge, 1902.

ABBREVIATIONS

B.H. = *Biblia Hebraica*, ed. R. Kittel, Stuttgart, 1937.
B.M. = Brooke–McLean (see above).
M.T. = Masoretic Text.
J.T.S. = *Journal of Theological Studies*.
T.L.Z. = *Theologische Literaturzeitung*.
Z.A.W. = *Zeitschrift für die alttestamentliche Wissenschaft*.

The usual abbreviations for the books of the Bible are used, except that, following the Septuagint, the books of Samuel and Kings are referred to as the four books of Kingdoms.

INTRODUCTION

THE larger part of the following chapters is devoted to a problem that even within the bounds of the Septuagint Pentateuch is somewhat special if not unique. It is true that the textual criticism of the Septuagint in general abounds with difficulties that are special when compared with the difficulties that attend the textual criticism of the New Testament; but these the Septuagint worker soon comes to accept as his ordinary meat and drink. They have arisen because the Septuagint is not an original composition but a translation, and a translation that has often been revised in order to make it represent the original Hebrew more faithfully. Origen's efforts in this direction are well known; but recent studies have made it clear that there were others before him who did similar, if not so consistent, work,[1] just as did yet others who followed him. Naturally such revisers would take as their standard the Hebrew text then current, interpreted according to the understanding of their own particular school. Then there were still other revisers who, when faced with differences between the Greek and their Hebrew *Vorlage*, made their correction by inserting not a fresh translation of the Hebrew, but renderings taken from the independent versions made by Aquila, Symmachus and Theodotion. In addition to all this, the Septuagint text has, of course, its full share of common mistakes and accidents such as befall all manuscript traditions, and is further complicated because the various types of text produced by the revisions have intermingled. The result is that the textual critic of the Greek Pentateuch has normally far more unravelling to do before he can hope to reach his original text than has his fellow-worker in the New Testament. Nevertheless, his difficulties up to this point remain in the field of the lower criticism, and actually they are not altogether such enormous obstacles as the mere description of them might lead one to suppose.

[1] For a list of the books in which it is now thought that pre-hexaplaric recensions are to be found, see P. Katz, *Studia Patristica*, vol. I, *Texte und Untersuchungen zur Geschichte der altchristlichen Literatur*, vol. LXIII, pp. 346 ff. (Berlin, 1957), and *Z.A.W.* vol. LXIX (1957), pp. 78f.

There are, however, certain passages in the Septuagint where the difficulties are abnormally great, because in them the Greek differs widely from the Masoretic Text, not in words and phrases only, but in the contents and order of whole sections and chapters. One such notorious passage is found at the end of the Book of Exodus. Not only do the Greek chapters here diverge widely in order from the Hebrew, but even the contents of some chapters differ remarkably. Some immediate idea of the differences can be gained by a glance at Origen's revision. He is easily able to alter the Greek order to correspond with that of the Masoretic Text, but when it comes to the differences of content, he has often to abandon all attempt at correcting the LXX text. Instead he simply leaves the LXX passage as he found it, and adds a full translation of the corresponding portion in the Masoretic Text. His result differs so much from the LXX text, that in Brooke–McLean's edition the readings of the Origenic text could not be exhibited as variants of the text of Vaticanus B, but had to be set out separately in an appendix.

It is at once apparent that we face here a problem that cannot be solved by textual criticism alone. Admittedly the pre-Origenic text, too, proves upon examination to have suffered much revision and many mishaps. But bad as is all this confusion in our manuscript evidence, it is only a superficial difficulty: the main problem goes deeper. The wide differences between the Greek and the Masoretic texts obviously date from times earlier than all our extant Greek evidence. In consequence the matter cannot be solved merely by a careful sifting of the manuscript variants; it requires wider methods of investigation.

The problem is thus special, but it is not of isolated importance or narrow interest. The inquiries it provokes strike off along roads that lead beyond the confines of lower criticism into fields of much broader interest: to trace, if possible, how the Greek and Hebrew texts of this particular part of Exodus came to stand in their present form, to discover why they differ so widely, and to decide, in so far as we may, to what extent each of them may claim in the closing chapters of the book to represent the older tradition. This was the problem of which Wellhausen said (*Jahrbb. für Deutsche Theologie* (1877), p. 419), 'Die Sache ist einer eingehenden Untersuchung bedürftig und würdig'.

CHAPTER I

THE PROBLEM DEFINED

THE latter half of the Book of Exodus, in both the Hebrew and the Greek Old Testament, is largely taken up with the account of the tabernacle. Chapters xxv–xxxi record the detailed instructions given by God to Moses for the making of the tabernacle, the tabernacle furniture and the priests' vestments. Chapters xxxv–xl relate in similar detail the carrying out of those instructions by the workmen until eventually the tabernacle is erected complete. For convenience we may call these the first and second accounts. In the first account the Greek follows the Hebrew fairly closely—and by the Hebrew we here mean the Hebrew of the Masoretic Text. In the second account the Greek departs widely from the Hebrew both in order and content.

The divergence is largest in the *order* in which the subject-matter is arranged. Most notable of all is the position in the record of the priests' vestments. The Hebrew relates their manufacture in ch. xxxix, the Greek in ch. xxxvi. The other major items, too, are differently arranged. The Hebrew order is: the tabernacle curtains, frames, veils and pillars (ch. xxxvi), the tabernacle furniture (ch. xxxvii), the court furniture and finally the court hangings, pillars and gate (ch. xxxviii). The Greek has: the tabernacle curtains, veils and pillars, followed immediately by the court hangings, pillars and gate (ch. xxxvii); and then the tabernacle furniture and the court furniture (ch. xxxviii).

Next the Greek *omits* certain major items. It has no record of the making of the eleven goats'-hair curtains, of the two sets of skin coverings, of the frames which formed the sides and back of the tabernacle, nor of the golden incense altar. In many other instances its account is drastically abbreviated or paraphrased. It describes, for example, the making of the ten linen curtains of the tabernacle in two verses (xxxvii. 1, 2) whereas in the Hebrew the details fill six verses (xxxvi. 8–13). On the other hand it sometimes adds pieces of information not given in the Hebrew, as, for instance, when it says in ch. xxxviii. 22: 'He

3

made the copper altar out of the copper censers which belonged to the men who rebelled with the company of Korah.'

The differences between the Greek and Hebrew are thus very large: there is nothing comparable in the rest of the Pentateuch. In addition to this there is a curious difference in the Greek of the first and second accounts. The words used in the second account to translate the Hebrew technical terms are often quite different from the words used for the very same technical terms in the corresponding section of the first account. No more need be said about this now, but it is a phenomenon that will later need close attention.

Now all these facts have long since been observed, and from them scholars have drawn far-reaching conclusions. W. Robertson Smith, for instance, in his book *The Old Testament in the Jewish Church*, pp. 124–5, says:

But there is one considerable section, Exod. xxxv–xl, where extraordinary variations appear in the Greek, some verses being omitted altogether, while others are transposed and knocked about with a freedom very unlike the usual manner of the translators of the Pentateuch. The details of the variations need not be recounted here; they are fully exhibited in tabular form in Kuenen's *Onderzoek*, 2nd ed., vol. I, p. 77, and in Driver's Introduction, pp. 37 *sq*. The variations prove either that the text of this section of the Pentateuch was not yet fixed in the third century before Christ, or that the translator did not feel himself bound to treat it with the same reverence as the rest of the Law. But indeed there are strong reasons for suspecting that the Greek version of these chapters is not by the same hand as the rest of the Book of Exodus, various Hebrew words being represented by other Greek equivalents than those used in the earlier chapters. And thus it seems possible that this whole section was lacking in the copy that lay before the first translator of the Law....Most modern critics hold chaps. xxxv–xl for a late addition to the text, and see in the variations between the Hebrew and the Greek proof that the form of the addition underwent changes, and was not finally fixed in all copies when the Septuagint version was made.....Those who hold that the Septuagint translators had to deal with a text that had been fixed and sacred for a thousand years, have a hard nut to crack in the wholly exceptional freedom with which the Greek version treats this part of the sacrosanct Torah.

H. B. Swete, in his *Introduction to the Old Testament in Greek*, p. 235, says:

It is clear from this comparison that both the Greek and the Hebrew follow a system, i.e. that the difference of sequence is due to a deliberate re-arrangement of the groups. Either the Alexandrian translator has purposely changed their relative order, giving precedence to the ornaments of the priesthood which are subordinated in the M.T. of cc. xxxv–xl, as well as in both texts of cc. xxv–xxx; or he had before him in c. xxxv ff. another Hebrew text in which the present Greek order was observed. Many O.T. scholars (e.g. Kuenen, Wellhausen, Dillmann) regard cc. xxv–xl as belonging to a 'secondary and posterior stratum of P'. Thus it is permissible to suppose that the Hebrew text before the original translators did not contain this section, and that it was supplied afterwards from a longer Hebrew recension of the book in which the last six chapters had not yet reached their final form. That the translation of these chapters was not made by the same hand as the rest of Exodus has been gathered from the fact that the Hebrew technical terms which are common to xxv–xxx and xxxv–xl are in certain cases differently rendered in the two contexts.

A. H. McNeile, in his commentary on the Book of Exodus (in the Westminster Commentaries series), pp. 223–6, endorses Swete's conclusions and adds a list of technical terms in which the LXX rendering of chs. xxxv–xl differs from that of xxv–xxxi.

But by far the most extensive work hitherto done on this problem[1] was published as early as 1862 by Julius Popper under the title *Der biblische Bericht über die Stiftshütte*. Though it is an exceedingly painstaking piece of work extending to some 212 pages of very close print with an appendix of specially arranged Hebrew text with notes extending to another 43 pages, it seems largely to have escaped the notice of British scholars. It is impossible here to summarize adequately Popper's long discussions of his predecessors in the field, and his own detailed arguments; where necessary the latter will be commented on later in their appropriate contexts. His main contentions, however, are as follows:

(1) Comparison of the two Hebrew sections relating to the tabernacle with the Samaritan text proves that the second Hebrew section is much later than the first (pp. 60 ff.).

---

[1] To the above list should be added the article by A. H. Finn in *J.T.S.* vol. xvi, pp. 449–82. For further comments on this article see author's preface.

(2) The second, later section is itself composed of two parts: the earlier part, marked by the recurrence of the formula 'as the Lord commanded Moses', chs. xxxv–xxxvi. 8 and ch. xxxviii. 21 to the end; the later part, chs. xxxvi. 8–xxxviii. 20, from which the formula is missing (pp. 140 ff.).

(3) The great divergence in the Greek extends from xxxvi. 8–xxxviii. 20; and that, because the LXX translators did not find in their Hebrew text the portion that is now xxxvi. 8–xxxviii. 20 in our M.T. In their Hebrew text, the account of the vestments followed immediately after xxxvi. 8—that is, the present Greek order follows what was originally the order of the Hebrew (pp. 151 ff.).

(4) Hence is explained the fact that the Greek of the second section translates the account of the priests' vestments in full—it is original LXX; but the Greek of xxxvi. 8–xxxviii. 20 abbreviates, paraphrases and has Targumic additions—it is a later addition to the LXX (pp. 151 ff.). Hence also the difference between the first section of the Greek and the second (xxxvii. 1–xxxviii. 27 Gk.) in the translation of technical terms (pp. 172 ff.).

(5) Even in this later addition, xxxvi. 8–xxxviii. 20, the Greek order, and not the Hebrew, is original (pp. 163–4).

(6) Within this broad scheme of earlier and later sections there are probably other strata of different ages. In particular, all the 'as the Lord commanded Moses' passages may not be of the same age (pp. 204 f.).

Popper, it will be seen, is far more precise and definite in his conclusions, as he is likewise more detailed in his handling of the LXX evidence, than are the British scholars. All agree that the second section in the Hebrew must be late; but not all agree exactly how much of the Hebrew of the second section was present in the Hebrew text of the LXX translators; and, in consequence, they are not equally definite as to how much of the Greek of the second section is original translation and how much is later addition. Nevertheless, their main conclusions are similar, and they all have in common as a part of their argument this appeal to the differences in the translation of technical terms. The use of technical terms, therefore, will provide a suitable starting-point from which to re-examine the whole problem.

Now Exodus is not the only book in the Pentateuch to contain technical terms. Numbers and, above all, Leviticus abound with technical details relating to the tabernacle, the offerings and the feasts. Here then we have opportunity to study over a wide area the normal style of the LXX translators and their practice with technical terms. It will provide a broad and safe basis for examining the apparently strange usage in Exodus, and will save us from the hasty conclusions into which some have been betrayed by too restricted an investigation.

CHAPTER II

THE TRANSLATION OF TECHNICAL
TERMS IN THE PENTATEUCH

THE manner of the translation of technical terms in the
Septuagint proves upon examination to be somewhat remarkable. A competent translation, when it comes to technical
terms, must choose its renderings with precise accuracy and
adhere to them with unvarying consistency, for inconsistency in
this regard cannot but cause confusion and misunderstanding.
The Septuagint surprisingly makes no attempt at a consistent
translation of technical terms; in fact its renderings are often so
varied that the variation cannot be due to carelessness,[1] but
must be the result of deliberate style. Such a curious phenomenon in an otherwise intelligent and on the whole competent
translation, as the Greek Pentateuch is, obviously calls for close
examination.

Now it is no new thing to observe that in the general run of
the narrative the translators have everywhere striven after
variety in the translation of non-technical terms, very much in
the manner of the English A.V. It is a characteristic feature of
the Septuagint, remarked upon by so many scholars[2] that a few
examples will here suffice to illustrate the point.

Genesis

קֶבֶר: xxiii. 4 τάφος, xxiii. 6 μνημεῖον.

וַיָּקָם שָׂדֵה: xxiii. 17 καὶ ἔστη ὁ ἀγρός, xxiii. 20 καὶ ἐκυρώθη ὁ ἀγρός.

מֵאָלָתִי: xxiv. 41 ἐκ τῆς ἀρᾶς μου, ἀπὸ τοῦ ὁρκισμοῦ μου.

וַיָּרִיבוּ: xxvi. 20 καὶ ἐμαχέσαντο, xxvi. 21 ἐκρίνοντο δέ.

בְּשָׁלוֹם: xxvi. 29 μετ' εἰρήνης, xxvi. 31 μετὰ σωτηρίας.

Leviticus

לִרְאוֹת: xiv. 36 ἰδεῖν, καταμαθεῖν.

עַם הָאָרֶץ: xx. 2 τὸ ἔθνος τὸ ἐπὶ τῆς γῆς, xx. 4 οἱ αὐτόχθονες τῆς γῆς.

יִמַּקּוּ: xxvi. 39 καταφθαρήσονται, τακήσονται.

---

[1] As Swete suggests: Introd. p. 329.
[2] See, for example, Swete's Introd. p. 328.

Deuteronomy

נֵלְכָה: xiii. 2 (3) πορευθῶμεν, xiii. 6 (7) βαδίσωμεν.

הַמֵּת: xxv. 5 τοῦ τεθνηκότος, xxv. 6 τοῦ τετελευτηκότος.

Such variation is, of course, deliberate. It shows that the translators were concerned to make their translation as readable as possible and aimed at a colourful rendering of the sense, rather than a dull, but exact, adherence to the letter. It is, in fact, what might be expected of good translators. But it is all the more startling to find such translators applying the same sort of variation to semi-technical and technical terms, which ought to be rendered with unvarying precision.

As a fair sample of their work in this connection we may take Leviticus: it is full of technical terms relating to the offerings and the feasts, and at the same time it is not embarrassed by complicated problems such as beset the technical chapters at the end of Exodus.

The following list will give some idea of the extent and thoroughness of the variation.

עֹלָה, burnt-offering: i. 3 ὁλοκαύτωμα, i. 4 κάρπωμα, i. 10 ὁλοκαύτωμα, i. 9 κάρπωμα, vi. 9 ὁλοκαύτωσις.

מִנְחָה, meal-offering: ii. 13 θυσίασμα, ii. 14 θυσία, xxiii. 13 θυσία, but in same verse θυσία is used for אִשֶּׁה.

אִשֶּׁה, an offering made by fire: i. 9 θυσία, ii. 2, 3 θυσία (though in ii. 3 θυσία also equals מִנְחָה), ii. 10 κάρπωμα, iv. 35 ὁλοκαύτωμα, xxiii. 36 ὁλοκαύτωμα, xxiii. 37 κάρπωμα (and in v. 37 ὁλοκαύτωμα = עֹלָה), xxiv. 7 προκείμενα, xxiv. 9 θυσιαζόμενα.

הֵנִיף תְּנוּפָה, to wave a wave-offering: vii. 20 (30) ἐπιθεῖναι δόμα, x. 15 ἀφόρισμα ἀφορίσαι, viii. 27 ἀνήνεγκεν...ἀφαίρεμα, viii. 29 ἀφεῖλεν...ἐπίθεμα, ix. 21 ἀφεῖλεν...ἀφαίρεμα, xiv. 24 ἐπιθήσει...ἐπίθεμα.

תְּרוּמָה, heave-offering: vii. 24 (34) ἀφαίρεμα, xxii. 12 ἀπαρχαί.

נְדָבָה, freewill-offering: vii. 6 (16) ἑκούσιον, xxii. 18 αἵρεσις, xxii. 23 σφάγια.

נֶדֶר, vow: xxii. 18 ὁμολογία, xxii. 21 εὐχή.

לֶחֶם, bread: xxi. 6, 8, xxii. 25 δῶρα, though in xxii. 18, 27 δῶρα is used for קָרְבָּן.

הִקְטִיר, to make to smoke, that is, to offer *by burning*, ii. 9 ἐπιθήσει, ii. 11 προσοίσετε, iii. 5 ἀνοίσουσιν.

9

yet הֵנִיף, which means to offer *by waving*, is likewise rendered: xxiii. 11 ἀνοίσει, xxiii. 12 φέρητε, xxiii. 20 ἐπιθήσει.

נִתַּח, to cut (a sacrifice) in pieces: i. 6 μελιοῦσιν, i. 12 διελοῦσιν, viii. 20 ἐκρεανόμησεν (a *hapax leg.* in the LXX).

נְתָחִים, pieces (of a sacrifice): i. 6 μέλη, i. 8 διχοτομήματα.

קֶרֶב, entrails: iii. 14 ἡ κοιλία, iv. 8 τὰ ἐνδόσθια.

כְּרָעַיִם, legs (of victims): i. 9 πόδες, iv. 11 ἀκρωτήρια.

דֶּשֶׁן, fat ashes: i. 16 σποδός, iv. 12 σποδιά, vi. 10 (3), 11 (4) κατακάρπωσις.

In view of these examples it is evidently insufficient to say that the translator has *failed* to translate his technical terms consistently. That would imply a certain carelessness, whereas the variation apparent in the above list is obviously the result of a very deliberate style. The fact is that, without regard for the technical character of these chapters, he has striven hard to turn them too into readable literature; and the varying translations of for instance כְּרָעַיִם and דֶּשֶׁן show how far out of his way he has gone to attain his end. With semi-technical terms variation does not matter; but that עֹלָה, מִנְחָה, אִשֶּׁה, תְּנוּפָה and תְּרוּמָה should be translated not only in various ways, but by terms that the translator uses interchangeably of now one and now another, and that no consistent distinction should be attempted between the verbs 'to offer', 'to offer by fire', 'to offer by waving', 'to offer by heaving', is evidence enough that the translator was completely indifferent to technical accuracy.

It will be observed that often his variations result from his giving technical terms a general sense according to the context in which he finds them. אִשֶּׁה means 'an offering made by fire', and the translation that is strictly (though not accurately) its Greek equivalent is κάρπωμα. But if the אִשֶּׁה in question is an עֹלָה, then he will translate אִשֶּׁה by ὁλοκαύτωμα, if it is a מִנְחָה, by θυσία, if it refers to the shewbread, by προκείμενα. Similarly תְּרוּמָה is normally ἀφαίρεμα, but can be represented by ἀπαρχαί; and לֶחֶם, bread, is rendered by δῶρα if it suits the context, even though δῶρα in a nearby verse represents קָרְבָּן. Singularly blessed by varying translations is the term תְּנוּפָה: it can be δόμα, ἀφόρισμα, ἀφαίρεμα or ἐπίθεμα according to the changing whim of the translator. But even where this obliteration of technical niceties does not lead to confusion in its immediate context (it is bound to create confusion in the end) it still remains that the translator has allowed himself a liberty which he would not have taken had he been at all concerned with technical accuracy.

An immediate result of these observations is that we must be wary of altering technical terms in the Hebrew text on the supposed authority of the Greek. In Lev. xxiii. 25, for instance, a note in *B.H.* suggests that ὁλοκαύτωμα in the LXX implies that the Hebrew text originally read עֹלָה, and not אִשֶּׁה, the present reading of the M.T.; but, of course, it does nothing of the sort.

Then this attitude of the LXX translators raises more general questions, such as, who were the translators and what was their general purpose? Swete has argued (Introd. p. 19) that the presence in the LXX of barbarous terms such as γιώρας, ἰν, σάββατα makes it unlikely that the LXX was an official translation authorized by Ptolemy. He claims that 'the whole style of the version is alien from the purpose of a book intended for literary use', and he concludes that the version arose out of the needs of the Alexandrian Jews and was made to be read in the synagogues. Was it then made officially by the Jewish religious leaders for their congregations? It is quite understandable that if the primary call for a translation was the practical necessity of having the Scriptures in the common tongue of the people, the religious leaders might well be content with a very modest literary style. But how can we reconcile with the efforts of religious leaders such laxity over technical terms, such deliberate striving after variety of expression even in technical contexts? Modern educated Jews are quite familiar with their religious terminology, even if they know no Hebrew; they talk freely of for instance 'mazzoth', or 'yom kippur'. The LXX translators *knew* Hebrew quite competently, could write idiomatic Greek when they pleased, and had presumably no less than average general knowledge. They were, moreover, sensitive enough to the Jewish religious feelings of the time to paraphrase rather than translate anthropomorphisms which the Hebrew employed in speaking of God.[1] Yet in Lev. xxiii we find some deliberate indifference to technical exactness that is really astounding. In *v.* 3 שַׁבַּת שַׁבָּתוֹן is translated σάββατα ἀνάπαυσις, in *v.* 32 σάββατα σαββατων. Again, the phrase מִמָּחֳרַת הַשַּׁבָּת, 'on

---

[1] See p. 20.

(or from) the morrow after the sabbath', occurs twice in this context. In *v.* 11 it is rendered τῇ ἐπαύριον τῆς πρώτης. In *v.* 15 it is rendered ἀπὸ τῆς ἐπαύριον τῶν σαββάτων; while in *v.* 16 עַד מִמָּחֳרַת הַשַּׁבָּת הַשְּׁבִיעִת, 'unto the morrow after the seventh sabbath', is translated ἕως τῆς ἐπαύριον τῆς ἐσχάτης ἑβδομάδος. So then, faced with שַׁבָּת and שַׁבָּתוֹן, the Greek within the compass of a few verses sometimes translates, sometimes transliterates and sometimes paraphrases. Now we may well imagine Jews of the Dispersion being indifferent to the technical terms of sacrifices which they could no longer offer; but are we to think that their official leaders were indifferent as to the exact translation of שַׁבָּת in passages of scripture that determined their annual feasts? Had they no recognized, official terminology? If they had, the translator (or translators) of Leviticus creates the impression that he deliberately varied it as often as possible and, at the expense of accuracy, attempted to make even Leviticus a 'readable' piece of literature. If then the LXX Leviticus be the official work of Jewish religious leaders, it casts an interesting light on the religious outlook of the Jews at Alexandria. They must have been widely different from their contemporaries in Judaea and from all orthodox rabbis the world through ever since.

Of recent times it has been suggested that the origins of the Septuagint were as follows. Before the LXX version was made there were in use a number of differing, partial translations made independently of each other for the practical purpose of helping the congregations at the synagogue services to understand the lesson. These, however, eventually created confusion in the minds of the people, as from time to time in the synagogues they heard read varying translations of the same passage of Holy Scripture. To end this confusion, a committee was authorized to revise these varying translations and incorporate them in an authorized version, which should then supplant all previous translations. As yet, of course, the suggestion, though attractive, remains an unproven theory; but when all the evidence for and against it is finally weighed, the observations of this chapter will have to be put in the scale against it. Admittedly, such an authorized committee may, like the translators of the English A.V., have deliberately varied its translations of ordinary words; but surely it could not have been indifferent to accuracy and consistency in respect of technical terms, if its aim were to end confusion in the minds of the people. It is in the matter of technical terms that confusion is the most readily caused by variation and inconsistency. It is, of course, possible to argue that a religious committee, aiming at uniformity in the synagogues, would be content if the official version were read everywhere, however inexact and inconsistent it was itself. But normally when religious leaders attempt to secure uniformity, they take special care that the technical terms of their religion should be everywhere uniform, particularly in Holy Scripture, which by its authority and frequent recitation will establish those technical terms in the minds and custom of the people. And with such a purpose it is very difficult to associate the literary style of the LXX Leviticus. Moreover, the variation in question is not a matter of textual variants;[1] so it cannot result from contamination between the Septuagint and previous translations. Nor can the variation be taken to indicate that the Septuagint is a patchwork of excerpts from previous translations; the variation enters into the woof and warp of the translator's style. Leviticus, at least, is a homogeneous translation.

Happily, the question of Septuagint origins is only incidental to this study. The evidence of 'style' is inconclusive. On the one hand the crude transliterations that occur here and there are inconsistent with a 'literary style'; yet on the other there seems in the many technical passages to have been a deliberate effort to produce a readable, rather than exact, translation. The question must remain open.

Finally, before we turn to the problems of technical terms in Exodus, it is a point worth noticing for future reference that this attitude to technical matters does not imply that the translators regarded these technical details of the Torah as less sacrosanct than the other parts. The same attempt at variety pervades all; it is just the fact that this same attitude was maintained towards technical details that strikes us as odd.

[1] In fact, of the five books Leviticus has the fewest sizeable variants.

CHAPTER III

SOME TECHNICAL TERMS RELATING TO THE TABERNACLE

THUS far we have examined the general style of the LXX Pentateuch and the translator's way with technical terms in Leviticus. The next step will be to investigate the style of Exodus, first generally and then specially in those technical passages which form the storm-centre of our problem. Before we take that step, however, it will be helpful if we can gain some idea of the objects to which the technical chapters of Exodus refer. There will be no need, of course, to enter here into a detailed description of every part of the tabernacle and its furniture; the interested reader will find such descriptions with diagrams in the commentaries. It will be sufficient if we understand what is meant by the Hebrew terms which the Greek either mistakes altogether or obscures by inconsistent translations. It is on these terms that much of the subsequent discussion necessarily turns. Fortunately the Hebrew, unlike the Greek, is consistent throughout in its use of these terms, so that it is easy to get a clear picture from the Hebrew before attempting to pick one's way through the confusion of the Greek.

1. THE GENERAL LAY-OUT

The tabernacle, then, was a small oblong building standing in a court. The court was marked off from the surrounding desert by linen curtains, hung from pillars which stood at suitable distances all the way round (xxvii. 9–19). The building was formed at the back and both sides by wooden frames (xxvi. 15–30). Across the front hung a large curtain to form a 'screen for the door'; it was upheld by five pillars (xxvi. 36, 37). The building was divided into two compartments by another curtain upheld by four pillars (xxvi. 31–5).

2. THE PILLARS

These four pillars were made of wood and covered with gold; they stood in bases of silver and had no capitals (xxvi. 32).

The five pillars at the door were likewise made of wood and covered with gold; they stood in copper bases and had capitals overlaid with gold (xxvi. 37, xxxvi. 38 M.T.).

The pillars which upheld the court curtains were only half the height, namely, five cubits; they stood in bases of copper and their capitals were overlaid with silver. These pillars are said by the Hebrew to be מְחֻשָּׁקִם with silver (xxvii. 17). It is not clear whether the Hebrew denotes an ornamental band round the pillar just beneath the capital, or whether it means a connecting rod running between the pillars. The R.V. rendering, 'filleted', follows the former view.

All the pillars were supplied with hooks from which their curtains were suspended. The Hebrew terms are: עַמּוּד, pl. עַמּוּדִים, pillar. אֶדֶן, pl. אֲדָנִים, base. רֹאשׁ, pl. רָאשִׁים, capital. וָו, pl. וָוִים, hook.

3. THE FRAMES

The frames that formed the back and sides of the building were, of course, completely different things from the pillars. The A.V. and the R.V. call them boards, but they were rather a kind of skeleton framework, light in construction, easily assembled side by side to form a wall, and easily dismantled when the camp moved. They were held in place, when assembled, by bars which were shot through rings fixed in each frame. They stood in silver bases; had no capitals, but were overlaid with gold[1] (xxvi. 15–30 (M.T. xxxvi. 20–34), xxxviii. 27). The Hebrew term consistently used is קֶרֶשׁ, pl. קְרָשִׁים, frame. The term for base is again אֶדֶן.

4. THE CURTAINS AND COVERINGS

The entrance to the court was called the gate, the entrance to the tabernacle the door. The curtains which hung at both gate and door were called screens: the Hebrew term is מָסָךְ (xxvi. 36, xxvii. 16).

The curtain which divided the building into two compartments was given a special name. It screened off from the holy place the holiest of all; it was the veil *par excellence*. The Hebrew term for it, פָּרֹכֶת, is applied to no other curtain (xxvi. 31).

[1] For full description and illustration see Kennedy's article on the Tabernacle in Hastings' *Dictionary of the Bible*.

Over the top, sides and back of the building was spread a series of four coverings.

(1) *Ten linen curtains*, richly embroidered, were sewn together into two sets of five curtains each, and the two sets were spread over the building and joined to each other by fifty golden clasps (xxvi. 1). In strict technical language it was these ten curtains that were called 'the tabernacle'—Hebrew מִשְׁכָּן—though the term is often used generally of the whole building. A clear example of the strict use of the term is seen in xxvi. 6: the two sets of linen curtains are joined together '*that the tabernacle may be one*'. The meaning of this last phrase is made even clearer if *v.* 11 is immediately compared with it. Verse 11 concerns the goats'-hair curtains, which are technically called 'the tent'. They were likewise made in two sets, which had to be joined together. The actual directions are: 'Couple the tent together that it may be one.' The term 'tabernacle' in *v.* 6, therefore, clearly means the ten linen curtains: it does not refer to the building; just as the term 'tent' in *v.* 11 refers to the goats'-hair curtains and not to the building.

The word for clasps is קְרָסִים; it should not be confused with קְרָשִׁים, frames. The word for curtains is יְרִיעֹת.

(2) *Eleven goats'-hair curtains* were sewn together into two sets, one containing five and the other six curtains. The two sets were joined together by fifty copper clasps, and were spread over the tabernacle: that is, over the ten linen curtains, to form 'a tent over the tabernacle'. The Hebrew term for these goats'-hair curtains is אֹהֶל, 'tent' (xxvi. 7–13). The word for 'clasps' is again קְרָסִים and for curtains יְרִיעֹת.

(3) *Rams' skins*, dyed red, formed a covering over the tent (xxvi. 14).

(4) *Sealskins* formed a covering over the rams' skins (xxvi. 14). The Hebrew word for both skin coverings is מִכְסֶה.

The importance of recognizing the strict technical meaning of the terms 'tabernacle' and 'tent' in this connection comes out clearly in M.T. xxxix. 33 ff. Here a list is given of all the articles which were made, as they were brought on their completion to Moses. It begins: 'And they brought the tabernacle to Moses, the tent, and all its furniture, its clasps, its frames, its bars and its pillars, and its bases; and the covering of rams' skins dyed red, and the covering of sealskins, and the veil of the screen.' The R.V. prints the word 'tabernacle' here with a small initial letter, and the word 'tent' with a capital. This gives the impression that 'tabernacle' refers to the whole construction, and 'tent' to the curtains; but it cannot be the right interpretation. The list is very detailed and includes separate mention of the ram-skin and sealskin coverings. Seeing therefore that these relatively unimportant coverings are separately mentioned, one may expect that the ten beautifully embroidered linen curtains and the eleven goats'-hair curtains will also receive separate mention; which they do if 'tabernacle' and 'tent' are allowed their strict meaning. If, on the other hand, 'tabernacle' is made to refer generally to the whole construction, 'tent' will have to do duty here for both the linen and the goats'-hair curtains, when, strictly speaking, it is the term that is used to *distinguish* the goats'-hair curtains from the linen. It is, of course, granted that the word 'tent' has elsewhere a wider significance, especially in such phrases as 'the Tent of meeting' (xxxix. 32); but in xxxix. 33 the stricter meaning is obviously the correct one.

5. THE FURNITURE

The furniture consisted of the ark and mercy-seat, the table of shewbread, the lampstand (R.V. candlestick), the golden incense altar, the laver and the copper altar (xxv. 10–40, xxvii. 1–8, xxx. 1–10, 17–21). The ark, table and incense altar were made of wood overlaid with gold; the copper altar of wood overlaid with copper. The mercy-seat and lampstand were made of gold only; the laver of copper only.

A few major points should be noticed here. First it is important to observe that there were, according to the M.T., two altars: the one for incense, the other for sacrifices. The incense altar stood in the first compartment of the building along with the table and the lampstand; in the lists in xxxv. 11–19, xxxix. 33–41, xl. 18–33 it is naturally grouped with these two vessels. The other altar stood in the court as did also the laver; in the lists it is naturally grouped with the laver. The design, size, position and function of the two altars were completely different.

The altar of sacrifice—commonly called the altar of burnt-offering, from the chief sacrifice that was offered upon it—was equipped with a copper grating, מִכְבָּר, that stood under the ledge, כַּרְכֹּב, which encircled the altar. Opinions differ on the function of this grating,[1] though it seems practically certain that it was not a fire-grate. It was probably detachable, for the lists mention both the altar and the grating.

Likewise the laver seems to have been made in two parts, for the lists speak of the laver and its base.

The incense altar was a far more delicate vessel than the altar of sacrifice. It had no grating, and unlike the copper altar it had an ornamental crown running round the top (xxx. 3).

The lampstand (xxv. 31) which supported the oil-lamps[2] consisted of a base—יָרֵךְ, a central shaft—קָנֶה—rising out of the base, and six branches—קָנִים—coming out of the central shaft. The Hebrew for shaft and branch is the same, for קָנֶה means literally a stalk, and both the shaft and the branches were hollow with solid joints here and there (the 'knobs' of *vv*. 31, 35) very much in the manner of a cane, or a stalk of wheat. In xxv. 31, however, this double use of קָנֶה has been misunderstood by the Samaritan (which reads the plurals of both יָרֵךְ and קָנֶה), the LXX and the A.V. The R.V. corrects the A.V.'s mistaken 'its shaft and its branches' and rightly has 'its base and its shaft'. The branches are then appropriately mentioned in *v*. 32. In strict terminology the lampstand refers to the base and central shaft and not to the branches. So when *v*. 33 has stated that there were three ornamental cups in each branch, the next verse begins 'And in the lampstand [i.e. in the central shaft] four cups'.

6. THE COURT HANGINGS

The court hangings were of linen. The only difference between them and the screen for the gate was that into the screen were woven blue, purple and scarlet colours. The height of the hangings and the screen was the same (M.T. xxxviii. 18). The word for hangings is קְלָעִים; it is quite different from יְרִיעֹת, which is used for the linen and goats'-hair curtains.

Enough has now been said to acquaint the reader with those parts of the tabernacle that will most frequently be met with in the following chapters. To help still further, there is a diagram and list of technical terms at the end of the book which can be unfolded and left open for quick reference.

---

[1] For instance, to support the ledge, to allow the blood to be dashed against the side of the altar, to catch the coals that fell off the altar, etc. For full discussion see the commentaries. [2] 'Candlestick' is an inappropriate term.

CHAPTER IV

THE GREEK EXODUS: THE FIRST SECTION

WE are now ready to examine the style of the translation of Exodus. As was mentioned in Ch. i, many scholars hold that chs. xxxv–xl are by a different translator from chs. i–xxxiv, and part of their reason for this view is that chs. xxxv–xl differ from chs. xxv–xxxi in their rendering of the same Hebrew technical terms. For the purposes of investigation, therefore, we shall divide Exodus into two sections, the first from ch. i to ch. xxxiv, the second from ch. xxxv to ch. xl, and we shall examine the style of each separately.

The first section contains narrative as well as technical passages. The following general features can be detected in the translator's (or, translators') style in the general narrative chapters.

(1) He deliberately varies his translation of ordinary words:

חָיָה: i. 16 περιποιεῖσθε, i. 17 ἐ3ωογόνουν.

צָפַן: ii. 2 ἐσκέπασαν, ii. 3 κρύπτειν.

עֲרַל שְׂפָתַיִם: vi. 12 ἄλογος, vi. 30 ἰσχνόφωνος.

וַיֶּחֱזַק לֵב פַּרְעֹה: vii. 13 καὶ κατίσχυσεν ἡ καρδία Φαραω, viii. 19 (15) καὶ ἐσκληρύνθη ἡ καρδία Φαραω.

וַיָּשֻׁבוּ הַמַּיִם: xiv. 26 καὶ ἀποκαταστήτω τὸ ὕδωρ.

וַיָּשֻׁבוּ הַמַּיִם: xiv. 28 καὶ ἐπαναστραφὲν τὸ ὕδωρ.

לְמִשְׁמֶרֶת: xvi. 32 εἰς ἀποθήκην, xvi. 33 εἰς διατήρησιν.

In this, his translation resembles that of the other books of the Pentateuch.

(2) He uses similar variety in the translation of technical terms:

אִשֶּׁה: xxix. 18 θυσίασμα, xxix. 25 κάρπωμα, xxx. 20 ὁλοκαυτώμοτα.

הִקְטִיר: xxix. 13 ἐπιθήσεις, xxix. 18 ἀνοίσεις, xxx. 7 θυμιάσει.

He is careless of technical accuracy:

θυσία: מִנְחָה xxix. 41, עֹלָה xxix. 42.

εἰσφορά: תְּרוּמָה xxx. 13, 15, כִּפֻּרִים xxx. 16.

In this he strongly resembles the translator of Leviticus.

(3) He can be quite idiomatic.

xvi. 36 הָאֵיפָה, τῶν τριῶν μέτρων.

xviii. 7 וַיִּשְׁאֲלוּ אִישׁ־לְרֵעֵהוּ לְשָׁלוֹם, and they asked each other of their welfare: καὶ ἠσπάσαντο ἀλλήλους.

xviii. 16 וְשָׁפַטְתִּי בֵּין אִישׁ וּבֵין רֵעֵהוּ, and I judge between a man and his neighbour: διακρίνω ἕκαστον.

(4) He can also be quite wrong.

xviii. 21 בֶּצַע (reward, bribe) ὑπερηφανίαν.

xxi. 22 וְלֹא יִהְיֶה אָסוֹן (and no mischief follow, R.V.) μὴ ἐξεικονισ-μένον.

xxv. 4 תּוֹלַעַת שָׁנִי (scarlet: literally, worm-scarlet) κόκκινον διπλοῦν.

(5) He has some noticeable Targumic paraphrases.

xxiv. 10 'and they saw the God of Israel'.
LXX 'and they saw the place where the God of Israel stood'.
xxiv. 11 'And upon the nobles of the children of Israel he laid not his hand: and they beheld God, and did eat and drink'.
LXX 'And of the nobles of Israel not one uttered a sound; and they were seen in the place of God, and did eat and drink'.

These general features show a mixed standard of performance: good, varied, idiomatic translation and deliberate paraphrase for the sake of religious scruple, side by side with neglect of technical accuracy, and thorough-going mistakes.

We turn next to see how the first section treats the technical terms of the tabernacle, and we are not now so surprised to find that the translation is frequently varied, often inconsistent and sometimes inexact. Even so, some of the inefficiencies and mistakes in translation are quite astounding.

First, the Greek makes no attempt to distinguish between the frames (קְרָשִׁים) and the pillars (עַמּוּדִים); it uses one term, στῦλοι, for both alike. This is remarkable, because the frames and the pillars were two of the most important structural components; and even if the translator could not picture the frames from the description of them given in ch. xxvi, the difference in the Hebrew terms ought surely to have made him realize that the frames were quite different things from the pillars.

Now these frames were equipped with 'tenons' or 'arms', יָדוֹת; they appear in the Greek as ἀγκωνίσκους in xxvi. 17, but everywhere else in the chapter they are referred to as μέρη. This is perverse; for having used one and the same term, στῦλος, for two completely different things, he now employs two different terms for the same thing. Moreover, the diminutive ἀγκωνίσκος occurs nowhere else in the LXX; so it would seem that the translator went out of his way to obtain the variation.

Again the tabernacle was equipped throughout with וָוִים, 'hooks' or 'pins', by means of which the curtains and hangings were suspended from the pillars. In xxvi. 32, 37 they are called κεφαλίδες, which is unfortunate, for the normal meaning of κεφαλίδες in a context like this would be 'capitals'. Indeed, it would seem that the translator intended the word to have its normal meaning despite the fact that it represents וָוִים; for if one read the Greek only of these verses, the juxtaposition of αἱ κεφαλίδες...καὶ αἱ βάσεις would lead one to give κεφαλίδες its normal meaning 'capitals' in contrast to the 'bases'. In ch. xxvii. 10, 11 the וָוִים are translated by κρίκοι, a much more reasonable rendering, which shows that the translator could not have been ignorant of the proper meaning of וָוִים. Nevertheless in the very same context, in v. 17, he reverts to the translation κεφαλίδες. This is truly an amazing performance; it is deliberate carelessness.

Some will object that the matter is explicable on other grounds: that the translator is not being careless at all, but is following a Hebrew text different from the M.T.; and that where he puts κρίκοι his Hebrew text had וָוִים, but where he puts κεφαλίδες his Hebrew read רָאשִׁים, and not וָוִים as the M.T. This explanation is very plausible, but closer inspection shows that for several reasons it cannot be right.

First, the translator of the first section is both in general and in this particular context following a Hebrew text that is demonstrably very close to the M.T.

Secondly, he has elsewhere been convicted of inaccuracy and inconsistency in the translation of technical terms; and we shall shortly discover more instances of first-class blundering.

Thirdly, it is exceedingly unlikely that any Hebrew text ever read רָאשִׁים instead of וָוִים in xxvi. 32, 37, xxvii. 17. These passages describe the veil pillars, the door pillars, and the pillars of the court and gate. xxvi. 32 in the M.T. says '...four pillars...overlaid with gold, their hooks of gold, upon four bases (sockets) of silver'. This means that the hooks were solid metal and so also the bases. The metal for the bases was silver; we are told in M.T. xxxviii. 25–7 where it came from. The metal for the hooks was gold, and it is quite understandable that such small articles should be made of solid gold. The LXX says: αἱ κεφαλίδες αὐτῶν χρυσαῖ καὶ αἱ βάσεις αὐτῶν τέσσαρες ἀργυραῖ, which makes it appear that these four pillars not only had capitals (which the M.T. nowhere says they did), but had capitals of solid gold! The same applies to the door pillars mentioned in v. 37, where again the LXX says αἱ κεφαλίδες αὐτῶν χρυσαῖ. Of these pillars the M.T. does say in xxxvi. 38 that they had capitals, but the capitals were *overlaid* with gold, not made of solid gold. The four veil pillars and the five door pillars were at least 15 ft. high, and capitals for them would be a considerable size. To overlay such capitals with gold-leaf—which is what the M.T. implies—would be costly enough; to make them of solid gold would involve an enormous expense, and is a most unlikely story. Even so the unlikelihood of this detail might not tell so heavily against it, if its presence did not rule out a very necessary and important item. The M.T. of xxvi. 31–7 is giving directions for veil and door-screen, and very naturally it mentions the hooks by which the two curtains are to be suspended from the pillars. These hooks are a necessary detail in this context, whereas the ornamental capitals for the door pillars are not so important and the M.T. does not mention them separately from the pillars. If the LXX translation κεφαλίδες represents a Hebrew text that read רָאשִׁים instead of וָוִים, that Hebrew text lacked completely all references to these hooks.

It is the same with the LXX use of κεφαλίδες in xxvii. 17. The passage is describing the court hangings and gate-screen and of course mentions the pillars on which they were hung. The M.T. describes the bases, fillets and hooks of these pillars, but again the ornamental capitals are not mentioned, either in the detailed description, vv. 9–16, or in the general summary in v. 17. The capitals are mentioned elsewhere in the M.T., in xxxviii. 19, and are there said to be overlaid with silver. The LXX in the detailed description of xxvi. 9–16 translates וָוִים correctly by κρίκοι, but in the general summary it has κεφαλίδες for וָוִים. Now it is quite credible that the hooks of the court pillars were made of solid silver, and that the capitals were, as the M.T.

states, covered with silver-leaf. But that some sixty court pillars[1] had capitals of solid silver, as the LXX states, is again an unlikely story. It is far easier to think that the LXX is here, as in so many other places, carelessly mistaken, than to suppose that it took this reading from a different Hebrew text.

Moreover, this same context provides other examples of our translator's inaccuracy. In xxvi. 36, in the directions for the screen for the door, he translates מָסָךְ by ἐπίσπαστρον, a word that occurs nowhere else in the LXX. In the next verse מָסָךְ occurs again, still referring to the door-screen; yet here it is translated καταπέτασμα. This certainly makes for variety, but καταπέτασμα was an unfortunate choice, for elsewhere in this same chapter, vv. 31, 33 bis, 34, 35, it represents פָּרֹכֶת—the veil— and פָּרֹכֶת in the Hebrew is a special term reserved exclusively for the curtain which divided the holy from the most holy place. The Greek thus obliterates an intended distinction. In xxvii. 16 another screen is mentioned, the screen for the gate. The Hebrew word is the same as for the door-screen, מָסָךְ,[2] and here there was no need to change the translation, ἐπίσπαστρον, which was used for the door-screen. The Greek changes it nevertheless; מָסָךְ here is rendered κάλυμμα; obviously the translator was determined to have variety.

Again, in the description of the two altars there occurs the phrase לְבָתִּים לְבַדִּים, 'for places for the staves'. In xxv. 26 (27) it is translated εἰς θήκας τοῖς ἀναφορεῦσιν, in xxx. 4 ψαλίδες ταῖς σκυτάλαις. A similar phrase in xxvi. 29, בָּתִּים לַבְּרִיחִם, 'places for the bars', is rendered εἰς οὓς εἰσάξεις τοὺς μοχλούς.

One more example may suffice to prove the charge of inconsistency against the translator. It concerns the translation of the points of the compass. In ch. xxvii. 9, 11, 12, 13 the

---

[1] McNeile has a curious mistake here, p. lxxx, l. 20. He gives the number of court pillars as 300; whereas 300 is not the number of pillars, but the measurement in cubits of the distance round the perimeter of the court. There were no more than 60 pillars at the most in the court. The mistake occurs in a passage where McNeile is collecting what he considers to be 'inconsistencies and obscurities...which render many important details impracticable'. The difficulty of transporting '300 pillars of the court, their bases of solid bronze, their pegs, cords etc.' is one of these 'inconsistencies' about which he complains; but the difficulty never really existed.

[2] The פָּרֹכֶת is also described as a מָסָךְ, for example xxxv. 11 (12); but no other מָסָךְ is described as a פָּרֹכֶת.

Hebrew quotes four points as follows: נֶגֶב־תֵּימָנָה, צָפוֹן, יָם, קֵדְמָה מִזְרָחָה. The Greek[1] translates them πρὸς λίβα, πρὸς ἀπηλιώτην, κατὰ θάλασσαν, πρὸς νότον. This seems very strange at first sight, but Popper, pp. 174–6, neatly explains the translations by giving them the values, south-west, north-east, north-west, south-east respectively. He then points out that in the corresponding part of the second section, Heb. xxxviii. 9, 11, 12, 13, Gk. xxxvii. 7, 9, 10, 11, the Hebrew terms are the same but the Greek translations different: πρὸς λίβα, πρὸς βορρᾶν, πρὸς θάλασσαν, πρὸς ἀνατολάς.[2] These translations give the Hebrew terms their normal meanings; and in the difference between the translations of the first and second sections Popper sees additional evidence for thinking that those sections were translated by different translators. It seems, however, to have escaped Popper's notice that three points of the compass are mentioned in ch. xxvi. 18, 20, 22. The Hebrew terms, נֶגְבָּה תֵּימָנָה, צָפוֹן, יָמָּה, are, apart from a small (and for our purposes insignificant) difference, the same as in ch. xxvii. The Greek, as it now stands, has πρὸς βορρᾶν, πρὸς νότον, πρὸς θάλασσαν; but obviously the order of the first two terms ought to be reversed. In fact, it is fairly certain that the Greek order was originally (and correctly) πρὸς νότον, πρὸς βορρᾶν, πρὸς θάλασσαν; for in v. 35 of this same ch. xxvi, πρὸς νότον stands for תֵּימָנָה, and πρὸς βορρᾶν for צָפוֹן. So then in ch. xxvi the Greek terms are, πρὸς νότον, πρὸς βορρᾶν, πρὸς θάλασσαν, in ch. xxvii for the same Hebrew terms they are πρὸς λίβα, πρὸς ἀπηλιώτην, κατὰ θάλασσαν. Yet no one has ever been rash enough to claim that ch. xxvi and ch. xxvii are by different translators; nor is there any MS. evidence to suggest that the terms in ch. xxvi result from a later revision of the Greek text. The difference between the terms in chs. xxvi and xxvii is just one more example of our translator's 'style'. We have already noticed that in this ch. xxvi he uses ἐπίσπαστρον and καταπέτασμα for מָסָךְ (vv. 36, 37), and ἀγκωνίσκοι and μέρη for יָדוֹת (vv. 17, 19, 20, etc.); and we may now add μέρος and κλίτος for צֶלַע (vv. 26, 27), though κλίτος is used in v. 28 for קָצֶה. He is consistent in his inconsistency!

[1] The B-text seems original here; the A-text has a later correction.
[2] The καὶ τὸ κλίτος τὸ πρὸς νότον... of BA* and some other MSS. in v. 9 is clearly an interpolation.

Inconsistency, however, is not his only fault; there are places where he is positively wrong. In *v.* 33 of this ch. xxvi, the Hebrew says 'And thou shalt put the veil under the clasps (תַּחַת הַקְּרָסִים), i.e. under the clasps which joined together the two sets of the tabernacle curtains, which were spread over the frames (see ch. xxvi. 1–7). The Greek has καὶ θήσεις τὸ κατα-πέτασμα ἐπὶ τοὺς στύλους which appears to be but a repetition of what *v.* 32 says (correctly) καὶ ἐπιθήσεις αὐτὸ ἐπὶ τεσσάρων στύλων. The Greek of *v.* 33 is, of course, quite wrong. *B.H.* has a note to the effect that the Greek ἐπὶ τοὺς στύλους implies in the Hebrew not תַּחַת הַקְּרָסִים but עַל הַקְּרָשִׁים, 'on the frames'. Now we cannot think that any Hebrew text ever read עַל הַקְּרָשִׁים, for to direct that the veil be put on the frames would not only contradict the direction of *v.* 32 that it be put on the pillars, but would be a senseless direction anyway. But it is quite possible that the translator mistook קְרָסִים for קְרָשִׁים; and his consequent translation ἐπὶ τοὺς στύλους would not appear to contradict the Greek of *v.* 32, for, as we have seen already, he translates both עַמּוּדִים (pillars) and קְרָשִׁים (frames) by the same word στῦλοι. So, however it is, the Greek is convicted of error.

Again in ch. xxvii. 14, 15, 16, the Hebrew gives the measure-ments for the gate-screen and for the hangings on either side: the hangings are each to be fifteen cubits, the screen twenty cubits. And so the combined length at the east end, where the gate is, will equal that of the west end, where the hangings are to be fifty cubits. The Greek in *v.* 16 gratuitously adds to the measurements the words τὸ ὕψος, 'in height', and so represents the gate as being twenty cubits high, that is twice the height of the tabernacle itself! And in *vv.* 14, 15 it has 'the height of the hangings (shall be) of fifteen cubits', which makes these hangings five cubits higher than the tabernacle. Once more it is very apparent that the Greek is simply mistaken; it is not dependent on some Hebrew text that was different from the M.T. For one thing it follows the M.T. in *v.* 18, where a summary of the measurements is given, and states that the height of the court was *five* cubits, thus openly contradicting its nonsense in *vv.* 14–16. And further: the purpose of *vv.* 14–16 in the M.T. is to give the width of the gate-screen and the hangings on either side, so that the position of the gate may be deter-mined. The measurements 15 + 20 + 15 add up to the known width of the court. The Greek, in making these measurements refer to height, is left without any measurement to determine the width of the gate or its position along the east side. Nor is there any evidence to suggest that the words τὸ ὕψος are a late addition to the Greek text. The translator has simply blundered, and it is quite understandable that a translator—especially our translator—should so blunder. It would be very difficult, however, to imagine a free Hebrew composition making such a mistake. If, however, we are asked to suppose that the Greek is following a 'mixed' Hebrew text that partly included the tradition which the M.T. later followed and partly other traditions, we shall observe that this supposed Hebrew text agrees with the M.T. here in all except *vv.* 14–16; that in *v.* 18 it contradicts what it says itself in *vv.* 14–16; and that it omits the information that is needed about the position and width of the gate. And having observed this we shall want to know who was stupid enough to compile such a Hebrew text and for what purpose it was compiled.

Meanwhile we must notice other glaring mistakes in this same context. In xxvii. 10 the Hebrew is giving directions for one long side of the court: it says: 'the pillars thereof twenty and their bases twenty of copper; the hooks of the pillars and their fillets of silver'. The Greek has καὶ οἱ στῦλοι αὐτῶν εἴκοσι καὶ αἱ βάσεις αὐτῶν εἴκοσι χαλκαῖ, καὶ οἱ κρίκοι αὐτῶν καὶ αἱ ψαλίδες ἀργυραῖ. This is a reasonable enough translation. We observe that the Greek equivalent for 'fillets' is ψαλίδες. The fillets were probably decorative bands running round each pillar underneath its capital. It is uncertain what the translator intended by ψαλίδες. The word is a good architectural term and could denote rounded mouldings; as such it well translates the Hebrew. But in xxx. 4 the translator uses ψαλίδες of the rings of the incense altar through which ran the staves that were used to carry the altar. This opens the possibility that the translator intended ψαλίδες in xxvii. 10 to mean rings, in spite of the fact that elsewhere (e.g. xxvi. 29) he uses δακτύλιοι for the Hebrew word for rings, טַבַּעַת. Maybe he thought that each of the court pillars was equipped with rings at the top just beneath the capital, from which the hangings were suspended by means of the hooks, that were fastened to the hangings and slipped through the rings. But however it is, ψαλίδες is certainly meant to represent the Hebrew חֲשֻׁקִים = fillets. In the next verse, xxvii. 11, the Hebrew gives directions for the other long side of the court; it says: 'and the pillars thereof twenty and their bases twenty of copper; the hooks of the pillars and their fillets of silver'. The Greek has καὶ οἱ στῦλοι αὐτῶν εἴκοσι, καὶ αἱ βάσεις αὐτῶν εἴκοσι χαλκαῖ, καὶ οἱ κρίκοι καὶ αἱ ψαλίδες τῶν στύλων καὶ αἱ βάσεις αὐτῶν περιηργυρωμέναι ἀργυρίῳ. Immediately we notice that the Greek mentions the bases twice, the second time in the list of things that were silver-plated. This makes nonsense: these bases were not silver-plated. If they were, why were not the bases on the other side (v. 10) silver-plated? It is possible, however, that αἱ βάσεις$^{2°}$ owes its presence in the text to a scribal error, although all manuscripts contain it. But the matter is not healed if we excise αἱ βάσεις, for the Greek still tells us that the hooks and the fillets were silver-plated, which just is not true. They were made of solid silver, as the Hebrew and Greek of v. 10 and the Hebrew of this verse tell us. The Hebrew expression is the same in both verses: וָוֵי הָעַמֻּדִים וַחֲשֻׁקֵיהֶם כָּסֶף. In v. 10 the translator was content to translate it to the effect that the hooks and fillets were of silver; in v. 11, apparently, he felt he must vary the expression. This is not all. In the summary of the instructions for the court in v. 17 the Hebrew tells us that all the pillars were filleted with silver. And so we get in the Hebrew the verb form corresponding to the noun, fillet, which occurred in vv. 10, 11. We might expect, therefore, that the Greek translation would be to the effect that the pillars were equipped with silver ψαλίδες. Instead, it has: οἱ στῦλοι...κατηργυρωμένοι—a translation so vague and inexact that it amounts to a positive mis-statement. Nevertheless the translator was presumably content to have gained another variation in expression—κατηργυρωμένοι instead of the περιηργυρωμέναι of v. 11.

When he comes to the main curtains of the tabernacle and tent (ch. xxvi) his love of variety again leads him astray. The ten tabernacle curtains were made of linen: the Hebrew word for curtains is יְרִיעֹת; it is correctly translated αὐλαῖαι. The eleven tent curtains were made of goats' hair, and the Hebrew word for curtains is the same as before. The translator here uses δέρρεις for יְרִיעֹת. Presumably he mistakenly thought that these curtains were made of goats' *skins*, and accordingly used

27

δέρρεις in spite of the fact that the Hebrew called them יְרִיעֹת. Goatskins, needless to say, would be vastly different things from curtains of woven goats' *hair*. Moreover when the Hebrew does speak of *skin* coverings, as in xxvi. 14, the word for covering is מִכְסֶה, and a word for skin is inserted. But perhaps it is too much to expect our translator to notice niceties of this sort.

The Greek also abbreviates and paraphrases. Of this there is a notable example in ch. xxviii where the Greek *vv.* 22–6 cover the Hebrew *vv.* 22–30. But in ch. xxv. 22 (23) the abbreviation misrepresents the facts. It says that the table was to be made of pure gold, whereas the Hebrew says that it was to be made of acacia wood and overlaid with pure gold. Now after all we have learned about the translator, his disregard for technicalities, his inconsistencies, his inaccuracies, his positive errors, it would be quite unsound criticism to follow his account of the table against that of the M.T., or to imagine that he was following 'another Hebrew text'.

We find, then, that in technical passages the translator of the first section of Exodus

(1) shows the same inconsistency in translating technical terms as does the translator of Leviticus, only in Exodus the inconsistency is even more glaring;

(2) is not only inconsistent in his use of technical terms, but is led by his carelessness to misrepresent and distort the account given by his Hebrew;

(3) often gives a translation that makes sense in the Greek, though it is not faithful to the Hebrew; but

(4) elsewhere patently contradicts himself within a comparatively short context;

(5) is not afraid to add to, abbreviate or omit details from the text as given by the Hebrew.

With this in mind we must now examine the second section so as to be able to compare it with the first.

CHAPTER V

THE SECOND SECTION:
PREVIOUS CONCLUSIONS

CHS. xxxv–xl of Exodus, which for convenience we call the second section, are altogether given up to technical matters. It is impossible, therefore, to compare the style of this section with the rest of the Greek Pentateuch in general, or even with the non-technical passages in the first section of Exodus, except in one particular. The Greek of the second section departs widely from the Hebrew in the order of the subject-matter (see Ch. 1). There is nothing comparable in the first section nor, indeed, in the other four books. Now if the Greek followed a Hebrew text, the order of which differed from our M.T. and was much the same as the present order of the Greek, there would be nothing here to suggest that the translator of the second section was not the same as the translator of the first, unless it could be proved that this other Hebrew text was not available to or used by the LXX translators. If, on the other hand, the translator of the second section rearranged the order to suit his own whim with no authority from his Hebrew text, his taking of this liberty, a far greater liberty than we find anywhere in the first section, might be held to argue a difference of translator between the first and second sections.

Strangely enough most scholars who hold that there is a difference of translator between the first and second sections deny that the translators have taken any such liberties, or that there have been serious accidental dislocations in the Greek text. On the contrary they maintain that the Greek order in the second section is original; that is to say, they think that just as the Greek of the first section followed a Hebrew text that was practically the same as the M.T., so the Greek of the second section followed another Hebrew text (or texts) that differed widely from the M.T. Swete (pp. 235–6), it is true, mentions the possibility that 'the Alexandrian translator has purposely changed' the order, but he does not adopt this view. He considers that while the order is deliberate and designed to give precedence to the ornaments of the priesthood, it is the order of a 'Hebrew recension of the book, in which the last six chapters had not yet reached their final form'. He hazards no guess as to the date and origin of this Hebrew recension, but he presumes apparently that it was not available to the LXX translators or else that they were not interested in it. Their Hebrew text according to him did not contain this section (chs. xxxv–xl); it was supplied afterwards from this Hebrew recension. Thereupon a hand other than that of the original translator rendered this last section into Greek and this rendering has come to stand in all our (non-hexaplaric) Greek manuscripts. Again Swete cannot tell us when this addition to the LXX was made, though it must have been very early to have found its way into all our extant manuscripts. Nor does he attempt to suggest under what authority it was made. The first section of Exodus he believes to have been translated to meet the need in the synagogues (see his p. 19). Was then this second section added in translation by later synagogue authorities? If so, and these authorities had come to the conclusion that their book of Exodus was not complete and that the people should hear the full story, one wonders how they were content to add such a miserably paraphrased and mutilated version of the story—a version that not only omits the incense altar, but also the tent of goats'-hair curtains and the frames; that mentions the ten tabernacle curtains but has no frames to support them.

But it will not be profitable to question Swete's suggestions too closely, for he cannot be taken as representative of even those scholars with whom he shares his main beliefs. In details they differ greatly. Swete, for instance, thinks that all of chs. xxxv–xl is secondary: Popper (pp. 151 ff.) will have it that all is original Septuagint up to the end of ch. xxxvi (Greek numbering). On this account it will not be fair to attempt a general summary of the views of scholars who have this minimum in common, that they consider that the present Greek order is derived from some Hebrew text, and that some part at least of the Greek chs. xxxv–xl is by a different translator from the first section of the book. The reader who wishes to study all the many suggestions that have been made is referred to the commentaries. It is possible, however, to pick out the main points that have led most of these scholars to their conclusions:

(1) Certain features about the Hebrew as we find it now in the M.T. and as compared with the Samaritan text.

(2) Belief that Hebrew passages showing strong priestly influences, and marked by a love and repetition of minute technical detail, come from late recensions made by a priestly caste. On that account the M.T. of the second section is regarded as a late recension because it gives an almost word-for-word repetition of the details of the first section.

(3) The fact that the tabernacle furniture is listed in the M.T. of the second section in a different order from what it is in the first section. And because the order in the second section seems more logical than that in the first, the first section is regarded as an early, the second as a late, recension.

With the foregoing considerations in mind scholars have come to the Greek and observed that

(4) The Greek of the second section, unlike the Greek of the first section and unlike the M.T. of both sections, puts the account of the priests' vestments *before* the details of the tabernacle. Hence they have concluded that this second Greek section is marked *by strong priestly influence, is based* (unlike the Greek of the first section) *on a late Hebrew text, and was translated some time later than the first Greek section.*

(5) In the first section in both Hebrew and Greek the incense altar is not mentioned along with the other furniture that stood with it in the holy place. It comes in much later (ch. xxx) after the description of the vestments and induction of the priests. This has been taken as evidence that ch. xxx in the M.T. is a late 'priestly' insertion and that there was once an early Hebrew tradition that knew nothing of an incense altar. But the Greek of the second section (unlike the M.T.) has no account of the making of the incense altar, and this is thought to be because this Greek was translated from a Hebrew text that followed the no-incense-altar-tradition. In other words, the Greek of the second section *followed an early tradition that was not under strong priestly influence.*

This result appears to contradict the deductions made from the position of the priests' vestments in the Greek second section (see (4) above); but it is explained by the supposition that there are not either in the Hebrew or the Greek just two strata, early and late, but several strata of different ages, intermingled with each other.

(6) The Greek of the second section gives a very abbreviated and mutilated account of the making of the tabernacle. From this it has been deduced that if the Hebrew underlying the Greek of the second

section were of the same quality and extent as the Hebrew of the first section, then either

(a) the translators did not regard the Hebrew of the second section as equally sacrosanct with that of the first, and therefore took liberties with it, or

(b) the translator of the second section must have been different from the first, seeing that he shows such a different attitude.

Alternatively, the suggestion is renewed that the Greek second section is following a different Hebrew tradition from that followed by the first; and from this again it is deduced that the Greek translation of the second section is later and by a different hand.

(7) The translation of Hebrew technical terms is different in the second section from what it is in the first; and this is taken as additional evidence that the two sections are by different translators.

Now the observations and findings noted under (1), (2) and (3) above are strictly speaking outside the scope of this essay. They are the special concern of Hebrew scholars. Only, since O.T. students have taken Hebrew source-theories to explain the state of the Greek translation and then have taken the Greek translation to corroborate the source-theories, this essay will have something indirectly to contribute to this field as it re-examines the Greek evidence and the use that has been made of it. But the main task will be to deal with the questions (4), (5), (6) and (7). They all concern the Greek text and the significance of its present state; and not until that state has been fully and accurately observed will it be safe to use its evidence as a guide to the problem of the Hebrew text.

It will be best, therefore, if we test first the conclusions that have been drawn from the translation of technical terms; for this is mostly a matter of collecting the facts properly and involves little subjective judgment. Thereafter we can proceed to questions of content, order, translation and revision.

The case for different translators, in so far as it depends on variations in translation of technical terms, has been well made out by McNeile, who states, p. 226:

The following are some of the technical terms in which the LXX rendering of chs. xxxv–xl differs from that of xxv–xxxi:

xxv. 12 (11) ἐλάσεις (R.V. 'cast'), xxxviii. 3 ἐχώνευσεν.
xxv. 14 (13), 27 (26) ἀναφορεῖς ('staves'), xxxviii. 4, 11 διωστῆρες.
xxv. 17 (16) ἱλαστήριον ἐπίθεμα ('mercy-seat'), xxxviii. 5 ἱλαστήριον.

xxv. 18 (17) χρυσοτορευτά ('of gold'), xxxviii. 6 χρυσοῦς.
xxv. 19 (18) κλίτος ('end'), xxxviii. 7 ἄκρον.
xxv. 37 λύχνοι ('lamps'), xxxviii. 16 λαμπάδια.
xxv. 38 ἐπαρυστήρ ('tongs'), xxxviii. 17 λαβίδες.
   ὑποθέματα ('snuff-dishes'), ἐπαρυστρίδες.
xxvii. 4 ἐσχάρα ('grating'), xxxviii. 24 παράθεμα.
xxviii. 11 γλύμμα ('graving'), xxvi. 13 ἐκκόλαμμα.
xxviii. 15 ἔργον ποικιλτοῦ ('the work of the cunning workman'),
   xxvi. 15 ἔργον ὑφαντὸν ποικιλίᾳ.
xxviii. 17 καθυφανεῖς ('set'), xxvi. 17 συνυφάνθη.
xxviii. 22 ἔργον ἀλυσιδωτοῦ ('wreathen work'), xxvi. 22 ἔργον
   ἐμπλοκίου.
xxviii. 32 ἵνα μὴ ῥαγῇ ('that it be not rent'), xxvi. 31 ἀδιάλυτον.
xxviii. 36 ἁγίασμα Κυρίου ('Holy to the Lord'), xxvi. 39 ἁγίασμα
   Κυρίῳ.
xxxi. 3 πνεῦμα θεῖον ('Spirit of God'), xxxv. 31 πνεῦμα.
xxxi. 4 ἐργάζεσθαι ('to work'), xxxv. 32 ποιεῖν.

The list is at first sight impressive, and the details it gives are,
apart from one or two minor blemishes, correct. It has nevertheless a grave weakness in that, as it stands, it tells only part of
the story. It compares single instances of renderings from each
section; it does not tell how many different renderings each
word may have elsewhere in the first section, or whether the
second section is consistent in its usage and always disagrees
with the first section over any one term. The list therefore needs
to be examined closely before the true value of its evidence can
be assessed. For this purpose I will take each instance he quotes,
giving the Greek reference each time (in the verse-numbers of
B.M.) with the Hebrew verse-numbers in brackets where
necessary.

יָצַק: xxv. 11 (12) ἐλάσεις, xxxviii. 3 ἐχώνευσεν.
But the first section uses χωνεύω for יָצַק in xxvi. 37, and no one
   would dream of suggesting that xxv. 11 and xxvi. 37 are by
   different translators.

בַּדִּים: xxv. 12, 13, 26, 27 (13, 14, 27, 28) ἀναφορεῖς, xxxviii. 4, 11
   διωστῆρες.
But (i) the first section also uses φορεῖς xxvii. 6, 7 and σκυτάλαι
   xxx. 4, 5, and this variety does not argue difference of translator;
      (ii) the second section uses ἀναφορεῖς xxxv. 11 (12), though
   usually διωστῆρες and once, mistakenly, μοχλοί xxxviii. 24 (7).

כַּפֹּרֶת: xxv. 16 (17) ἱλαστήριον ἐπίθεμα, xxxviii. 5 (xxxvii. 6) ἱλαστήριον.
But in xxv. 17, 18, 19, 20, 21 (18, 19, 20, 21, 22) the first section has plainly ἱλαστήριον.

זָהָב מִקְשָׁה: xxv. 17 (18) χρυσοτορευτά ('of gold'), xxxviii. 6 (xxxvii. 7) χρυσοῦς.
But (i) only B*ob₂ read χρυσοτορευτά; the majority have χρυσᾶ τορευτά;[1]

(ii) in xxxviii. 6 the Greek is deliberately abbreviated. Else-where the second section uses στερεός for מִקְשָׁה, for example, xxxviii. 14 (xxxvii. 17). This admittedly is different from the τορευτός of the first section; but Numbers uses στερεά of the lamp-stand in ch. viii. 4 and ἐλατάς of the trumpets in ch. x. 2 though the M.T. has מִקְשָׁה in both places. Shall we argue different translators for these two chapters in Numbers?

קָצָה: xxv. 18 (19) κλίτος ('end'), xxxviii. 7 ἄκρον.
But (i) the first section has μέρος for קָצָה in xxvi. 4;
(ii) the first section uses κλίτος for פַּעֲמֹתָיו in xxv. 11 (12), for צֶלַע in xxv. 11 (12), for צַד in xxv. 31 (32), for פֵּאָה in xxvi. 18, for קָצֶה in xxvi. 28, for כָּתֵף in xxvii. 14;
(iii) and in xxv. 31 (32), though κλίτος is used for צַד, the plural of צַד in this same verse is translated πλαγίων.
In the midst of such variety it is doubtful whether the difference between xxv. 18 and xxxviii. 7 has any significance.

——: xxv. 37 λύχνοι ('lamps'), xxxviii. 16 λαμπάδια.
λύχνοι translates נֵרֹת; but whatever λαμπάδια is meant to represent (גְּבִיעִים or פֶּרַח), it does not represent נֵרֹת, for the second section uses λύχνοι for נֵרֹת (xxxviii. 17). McNeile has made a mistake here.

מֶלְקָחַיִם: xxv. 38 ἐπαρυστήρ, xxxviii. 17 λαβίδες. The word is not elsewhere translated in the Greek Exodus. It is therefore impos-sible to compare the first section usage in other places. Here then is an unrelieved difference between the first and second sections. But we may note that
(i) ἐπαρυστήρ is a mistaken translation: the article referred to is not a bowl, but a pair of tongs or snuffers;
(ii) λαβίδες is correct, and is the translation given in Num. iv. 9, II Chron. iv. 21, Isa. vi. 6;

[1] Katz suggests that the Hebrew indicates an original τορ⟨ν⟩ευτ-, 'turned-work' (this suggestion and the evidence on which it is based are given in an as yet unpublished work).

(iii) ἐπαρυστήρ is not used elsewhere in the LXX, nor anywhere else in Greek. There are five instances of ἐπαρυστρίς which too is peculiar to the LXX. In III Kingd. vii. 35 (49) it represents the same מֶלְקָחַיִם; so III Kingd. agrees with the first section here.[1]

מַחְתָּה: xxv. 38 ὑποθέματα ('snuff-dishes'), xxxviii. 17 ἐπαρυστρίδες. But (i) ὑποθέματα is a *hapax leg.* in the LXX. Aquila uses it for מְכֹנוֹת 'bases', III Kingd. vii. 27 (14), which would seem to be its proper meaning;

(ii) Num. iv. 9 agrees with the second section in having ἐπαρυστρίδες for מַחְתֹּת;

(iii) it is instructive to compare the translation of מָסָךְ. As we have already seen, the first section in xxvi. 36 uses ἐπίσπαστρον which also is a *hapax leg.* in the LXX (though used by Symmachus and Theodotion). Yet in the very next verse, 37, he uses κατα-πέτασμα for מָסָךְ. On analogy then, if מַחְתָּה had occurred again in the first section in connection with the lampstand, it is probable that the first section would not have used ὑποθέματα again, but one of the more usual terms.

מִכְבָּר: xxvii. 4 ἐσχάρα ('grating'), xxxviii. 24 παράθεμα. These are definitely different. ἐσχάρα is a grate in the sense of a hearth; παράθεμα simply means an appendage. It is tempting to think that περίθεμα, the reading of AFM alii in xxxviii. 24, is the correct one. It makes better sense. But the account of the copper altar is one of those parts in which the two accounts differ widely in the Greek in other respects than language. It must be examined in detail later.

פִּתּוּחֵי: xxviii. 11 γλύμμα ('graving'), xxxvi. 13 (xxxix. 6) ἐκκό-λαμμα. The full phrase is פִּתּוּחֵי חֹתָם. It is variously translated in both sections: xxviii. 11 γλύμμα σφραγῖδος, xxviii. 21 γλυφαὶ σφραγίδων, xxviii. 32 (36) ἐκτύπωμα σφραγῖδος, xxxvi. 13 (xxxix. 6) ἐκκόλαμμα σφραγῖδος, xxviii. 21 (xxxix. 14) ἐνγεγραμ-μένα εἰς σφραγῖδας, xxviii. 39 (xxxix. 30) ἐκτετυπωμένα σφραγῖδος; but when the translations in the first section are not twice the same in one chapter, it is difficult to deduce much from the fact that the translations in the second section are different. Moreover the first

---

[1] επαρυστρις B] επαρυστριδας rell. This acc. plur. ἐπαρύστρεις is consistent with θερμάστρεις which occurs twice in the same chapter, 26 (40) and 31 (45). Moreover, it was in Origen's *Vorlage* and was strangely misunderstood by him. For particulars, I refer to P. Katz, 'Das Problem des Urtextes der Septuaginta', *Theol. Zeitschr.* v (1949), p. 9='The Recovery of the Original Septuagint' (*Actes du premier Congrès de la Fédération Internationale des Associations d'Etudes Classiques*, Paris, 1951), pp. 170f.; *T.L.Z.* (1954), p. 241.

section does use the verb form κεκολαμμένη to translate חָרוּת 'engraved', xxxii. 16.

מַעֲשֵׂה חֹשֵׁב: xxviii. 15 ἔργον ποικιλτοῦ, xxxvi. 15 (xxxix. 8) ἔργον ὑφαντὸν ποικιλίᾳ. But the full evidence is: xxvi. 1 ἐργασίᾳ ὑφάντου, xxvi. 31 ἔργον ὑφαντόν, xxviii. 6 ἔργον ὑφαντόν (-ου Be) ποικιλτοῦ, xxviii. 15 ἔργον ποικιλτοῦ, xxxvi. 10 (xxxix. 3) ἔργον ὑφαντόν, xxxvi. 15 (xxxix. 8) ἔργον ὑφαντὸν ποικιλίᾳ, xxxvii. 3 (xxxvi. 35) ἔργον ὑφάντου. It would be difficult to argue difference of translators from a list like this. Moreover מַעֲשֵׂה רֹקֵם is translated: xxvi. 36 ἔργον ποικιλτοῦ, xxxvi. 37 (xxxix. 29) ἔργον ποικιλτοῦ. So the use of ποικιλτοῦ for חֹשֵׁב in xxviii. 15 is really another inconsistency in the use of technical terms.

מִלֵּא: xxviii. 17 καθυφανεῖς ('set'), xxxvi. 17 (xxxix. 10) συνυφάνθη. But (i) the difference is only in the preposition;

(ii) compare the translations of מִלֻּאִים. The first section has xxv. 6 (7) εἰς τὴν γλυφήν. The second section likewise has εἰς τὴν γλυφήν in xxxv. 8 (9), but a few verses later, in xxxv. 27, it has the altogether different τῆς πληρώσεως. Will it be claimed that xxxv. 8 is by one translator and xxxv. 27 by another?

מַעֲשֵׂה עֲבֹת: xxviii. 22 ἔργον ἁλυσιδωτοῦ, xxxvi. 22 (xxxix. 15) ἔργον ἐμπλοκίου. But the first section is not consistent: it has ἔργον πλοκῆς in xxviii. 14.

לֹא יִקָּרֵעַ: xxviii. 28 (32) ἵνα μὴ ῥαγῇ, xxxvi. 31 (xxxix. 23) ἀδιάλυτον. But compare the first sections ἀκίνητοι for לֹא יָסֻרוּ in xxv. 14 (15). It is in exactly the same style as ἀδιάλυτον of xxxvi. 31.

קֹדֶשׁ לַיהוה: xxviii. 32 (36) ἁγίασμα Κυρίου, xxxvi. 39 (xxxix. 30) ἁγίασμα Κυρίῳ. But it is doubtful whether this difference has any significance.

רוּחַ אֱלֹהִים: xxxi. 3 πνεῦμα θεῖον, xxxv. 31 πνεῦμα. But McNeile is following Swete's text. Only B* omits θεῖον in xxxv. 31.

לַעֲשׂוֹת: xxxi. 4 ἐργάζεσθαι ('to work'), xxxv. 32 ποιεῖν. It is, perhaps, just possible that this difference is significant; but with ποιεῖν in xxxv. 32 compare ἐργαζέσθωσαν and ἐν τοῖς ἐργαζομένοις in xxxvi. 6, 8.

So, then, examination of McNeile's list in the light of all the evidence, and in the light of the first section's attitude to technical terms, reveals that the differences are neither so many nor by any means so significant as would at first appear. Very few of them, perhaps only those relating to the lampstand and the

copper altar, could fairly be taken to argue difference of translator. In fact, thoroughgoing variety in the translation of
technical terms is so marked a feature of LXX style in Leviticus
and the first section of Exodus that the differences between
the first and second sections of Exodus might well be taken *prima
facie* to argue homogeneity of style rather than the reverse.

On the other hand, while scholars have emphasized differences
which are, in fact, largely insignificant, they have overlooked
striking similarities. The translation of אֵפֹד, ἐπωμίς, for instance,
is, as one might expect, the same in both sections. But in the
description of its details the word כָּתֵף occurs; for this the
first section, xxviii. 7, has, confusingly enough, ἐπωμίς again; so
has the second section, xxxvi. 11 (xxxix. 4)! It may, perhaps,
be argued that the translator of the second section deliberately
copied the translation of the first section to make his part appear
homogeneous with the first part. Why, then, did he not copy the
many other technical terms? A deliberate 'copier' would
certainly aim at thorough agreement here.

Again, just as the first section makes no attempt by its terms to
distinguish the veil, פָּרֹכֶת, from the screens for the door and gate,
so the second section likewise uses καταπέτασμα both of the
פָּרֹכֶת xxxvii. 3 (xxxvi. 35) and of the gate-screen, מָסָךְ xxxvii. 16
(xxxviii. 18).

Then we noticed (p. 27) how the first section ran into trouble
over the rendering of the verb and noun, fillet. Its noun for
fillet was ψαλίς (xxvii. 10); it stated (quite wrongly) that the
ψαλίδες were περιηργυρωμέναι ἀργυρίῳ (xxvii. 11); and where
the Hebrew (xxvii. 17) said that the pillars were מְחֻשָּׁקִים כֶּסֶף,
filleted with silver, it had οἱ στῦλοι...κατηργυρωμένοι ἀργυρίῳ
(again quite wrongly). The corresponding passage in the second
section is xxxvii. 15, 17, 18 (xxxviii. 17, 19, 20) and it presents
two interesting points. The M.T. (xxxviii. 17) has 'the hooks of
the pillars and their fillets of silver'. The Greek (xxxvii. 15) joins
the Samaritan text in having plainly 'their hooks of silver'; and
the word for hooks is ἀγκύλαι and not as in xxvii. 10, 11 κρίκοι.
Here then is a difference in translation between the sections.
The Hebrew proceeds (xxxviii. 17) 'the overlaying of their
capitals of silver and all the pillars of the court were filleted with
silver', וְצִפּוּי רָאשֵׁיהֶם כֶּסֶף וְהֵם מְחֻשָּׁקִים כֶּסֶף כֹּל עַמֻּדֵי הֶחָצֵר. For
this the Greek has καὶ αἱ κεφαλίδες αὐτῶν περιηργυρωμέναι

ἀργυρίῳ καὶ οἱ στῦλοι περιηργυρωμένοι ἀργυρίῳ πάντες οἱ στῦλοι τῆς αὐλῆς; and the position of the last five words in the Greek shows that the Greek is following a text very similar to, if not the same as, the M.T. The use of περιηργ- for the silver-plating, צִפּוּי, is very natural; but the use of περιηργ- again for the silver filleting, מְחֻשָּׁקִים, shows either carelessness or mis-understanding. The rendering is repeated in xxxvii. 17, 18 where for the Hebrew (xxxviii. 19) וְצִפּוּי רָאשֵׁיהֶם וַחֲשֻׁקֵיהֶם כָּסֶף the Greek has καὶ αἱ κεφαλίδες αὐτῶν περιηργυρωμέναι ἀργυρίῳ καὶ αὐτοί (referring to the στῦλοι) περιηργυρωμένοι ἀργυρίῳ. Now whether this rendering of מְחֻשָּׁקִים and חֲשֻׁקִים arises from carelessness or misunderstanding—and it must be one or the other, seeing that it is not accurate—it remarkably resembles the similarly mistaken or careless translation οἱ στῦλοι... κατηργυρωμένοι ἀργυρίῳ in xxvii. 17.

So far then as the translation of technical terms can guide us, we find

(1) that the differences so much spoken of by scholars are not as many or as significant as hitherto thought;

(2) what differences there are would be insufficient by themselves to prove difference of translator; rather might they be taken as a feature of LXX style;

(3) there are striking similarities between the two sections.

And this strange combination of similarity and dissimilarity could easily be explained if both sections were (for the most part) by the same translator: it is his normal style.[1]

Now Popper does, in fact, claim that a good deal of the second section is by the same translator as the first. He argues that the 'as the Lord commanded Moses' passages in the second section lay before the original LXX translators, but what is now xxxvi. 8–xxxviii. 20 in the M.T. was missing from the Hebrew text which they used (see Popper, pp. 151–4). He points out that the translation of the priests' vestments in the second section, Gk. xxxvi. 8–40, Heb. xxxix. 1–31, is in full, and in the same style as the first section; but that the translation of what is now xxxvi. 8–xxxviii. 20 in the M.T. is very free and abbreviated in the Greek, and was added later. So also he

---

[1] Finn, pp. 451–6, gives many other striking examples of similarity between the two sections. Many of them, however, come from ch. xxxvi (Gk.) which Popper, at least, admits is original LXX anyway.

accounts for the order of the Greek. The Hebrew of chs. xxxvi. 8 to the end is composed of two parts: the older part, ch. xxxix. 1 to the end,[1] the later part, chs. xxxvi. 8–xxxviii. 20. In the Hebrew text which the original translators used, what is now xxxix. 1 followed immediately upon xxxvi. 8, and the translators have preserved this order; what is now xxxvi. 8–xxxviii. 20 was missing from their Hebrew text, and when it was eventually added in the Greek, it was placed after the account of the priests' vestments.

Popper's explanation, however, is itself not without serious difficulties. Admittedly the Greek account of the vestments in ch. xxxvi is in a very different style from the account of the tabernacle furniture in ch. xxxviii: the former renders the Hebrew fully, the latter abbreviates heavily, adds information not in the Hebrew, and in one part, xxxviii. 18–20, does not appear to be following a Hebrew text at all. But ch. xxxix. 33– the end of ch. xl in the Hebrew is an 'as the Lord commanded Moses' passage and forms part of the older Hebrew text which, according to Popper, lay before the original translators. Yet this passage in the Greek (ch. xxxix. 14–the end of ch. xl) differs in style, not so much as ch. xxxviii, but very noticeably nevertheless, from the Greek account of the vestments in ch. xxxvi. It abbreviates, omits, and changes the order of some verses. At the same time the style of this passage strikingly resembles that of the Greek ch. xxxvii which is *not* an 'as the Lord commanded Moses' passage, but translates portions of the Hebrew (xxxvi. 8, 9, 35–8, xxxviii. 9–20) which, according to Popper, did not lie before the original translators; ch. xxxvii, too, omits and abbreviates, though it follows its Hebrew far better than does ch. xxxviii.

So, then, not all of what Popper claims as the older Hebrew text which lay before the original translators is translated with the same fulness and faithfulness; and not all of what he claims as the later addition is translated with the same freedom. Obviously these six Greek chapters are not homogeneous; but Popper's analysis and explanation are inadequate, and we must, therefore, examine the evidence afresh for ourselves.

[1] I.e., in view of p. 143, l. 8f. and p. 146, para. 4, the end of the book. On p. 151, l. 29, it is strangely limited to the end of ch. xxxix, and on p. 186 still further to ch. xxxix. 1–31.

CHAPTER VI

THE SECOND SECTION: FRESH CONCLUSIONS

I. CONTRADICTIONS BETWEEN CH. XXXVIII AND CH. XXXVII

THE first thing to notice is that ch. xxxviii positively contradicts ch. xxxvii. The Greek of ch. xxxviii says in *v.* 20 οὗτος ἐχώνευσεν τὰς κεφαλίδας τὰς ἀργυρᾶς τῆς σκηνῆς, καὶ τὰς κεφαλίδας τὰς χαλκᾶς τῆς θύρας τῆς σκηνῆς καὶ τῇ πύλῃ (or τῆς πύλης) τῆς αὐλῆς.[1] This, given its natural meaning, is 'He cast the silver capitals of the tabernacle and the copper capitals of the door of the tabernacle and for the gate of the court'. There is no Hebrew behind this and it is sheer nonsense. There were no silver capitals inside the tabernacle, and the capitals of the door pillars were covered with gold, not cast out of copper; and likewise the capitals of the gate pillars were not cast out of copper, but covered with silver. Moreover it cannot be argued that the second section is following a Hebrew tradition that was different from the tradition followed by the first section: the second section itself in xxxvii. 6 (xxxvi. 38) says of the pillars of the door of the tabernacle καὶ τὰς κεφαλίδας αὐτῶν κατεχρύσωσαν, and of the pillars of the court-gate, xxxvii. 17 (xxxviii. 19), καὶ αἱ κεφαλίδες αὐτῶν περιηργυρωμέναι ἀργυρίῳ. This agrees with the first section and with the Hebrew everywhere, but it means that there is a blatant contradiction between chs. xxxvii and xxxviii. It is difficult, therefore, to think that this part of ch. xxxviii is by the same translator as ch. xxxvii. In spite of all the inconsistencies and inaccuracies which we have noticed in the translation of technical terms, the Greek has not hitherto so blatantly contradicted itself. Moreover the whole thing is so gratuitous. The Greek is not normally given to unwarranted

---

[1] It is impossible to read with Bahqru τὴν πύλην. 'He cast...the gate' would be nonsense: the gate itself was an opening screened by curtains hanging on four pillars. We must read either τῆς πύλης with F¹?ᵃ? bdptxa₂, thus giving πύλης the same construction as τῆς θύρας, or else τῇ πύλῃ with the majority, construing it 'He cast...capitals...for the gate'.

repetition; rather does it abbreviate and omit. Yet although the information regarding these capitals has already been given correctly, following the Hebrew, in ch. xxxvii, ch. xxxviii, apparently following no Hebrew, needlessly repeats the information with these contradictory variations. It also repeats, in *v.* 18, the overlaying of the veil pillars with gold (cf. xxxvii. 4).

2. HOWLERS IN *vv.* 18–20 OF CH. XXXVIII

But this is not all. Ch. xxxviii contains two howlers, the origin of which it is fairly easy to detect. It says, in *v.* 18, οὗτος περιηργύρωσεν τοὺς στύλους, καὶ ἐχώνευσεν τοῖς στύλοις (A-text) δακτυλίους χρυσοῦς καὶ ἐχρύσωσεν τοὺς μοχλοὺς χρυσίῳ.... Now we have seen how the Greek uses στῦλοι for both the קְרָשִׁים (frames) and the עַמּוּדִים (pillars); but the order and information in this verse, στύλους...δακτυλίους...μοχλούς, shows conclusively that the στῦλοι in question are the frames; and yet the Greek here says 'He covered them with *silver*'!

The Greek of the first section and the Hebrew everywhere have it that the frames were covered with gold. McNeile, p. 172, considers that xxxviii. 18 represents a divergent tradition in which the frames *were* covered with silver. But if it were so, and if the translator of ch. xxxviii realized that the στῦλοι were the קְרָשִׁים = frames, seeing no description at all had yet been given of the στῦλοι = קְרָשִׁים in this second section, why did he not describe their making and what they were for? Why merely describe their covering with silver?

The far more likely explanation is this: this part of ch. xxxviii was not compiled by the translator of the first section, nor by the translator of the bulk of the second section; but whoever the compiler was, he copied a good deal of his information from the *Greek* of the first and second sections without very close reference to the Hebrew. The Hebrew places the account of the making of the frames directly after the curtains and coverings of the tabernacle. They ought therefore to come in the Greek in ch. xxxvii; but the Greek entirely omits them, although it mentions the pillars of the veil, door, court and court-gate. In fact, if one examines the lists in the second section, one finds that the second section consistently omits all reference to the στῦλοι = frames. Now xxxviii. 18 does mention the στῦλοι = frames, but the probability is that it has mistaken these στῦλοι for the στῦλοι = pillars. In xxvii. 17 the Hebrew says that all the pillars of the court were to be מְחֻשָּׁקִים כֶּסֶף. The Greek has στῦλοι . . . κατηργυρωμένοι ἀργυρίῳ. Likewise in xxxvii. 15 for the same Hebrew (xxxviii. 17) the Greek has στῦλοι περιηργυρωμένοι ἀργυρίῳ. The translation is not very accurate, as we have seen (p. 27), but it is consistent, apart from the small change of preposition in the verb. So when ch. xxxviii says in v. 18 περιηργύρωσεν τοὺς στύλους without having described their construction and without distinguishing them as either τῆς σκηνῆς or τῆς αὐλῆς, it seems probable that it is copying the Greek of chs. xxvii and xxxvii, not realizing that those two chapters are describing στύλους = pillars, while itself is referring to στύλους = frames. It is, of course, a mistake that would not be made by anyone who was following a Hebrew text of any kind, but it could easily be made by someone reading the Greek, which makes no attempt in its translation to distinguish between קְרָשִׁים and עַמּוּדִים, but calls both alike στῦλοι.

Moreover a second howler occurs here that confirms this explanation as the true one. Verses 19 and 20 of ch. xxxviii collect together bits and pieces of information that in the full accounts, both Hebrew and Greek, are widely separated; and all the details concern metalwork. Verse 19 describes the various metal hooks that were made: οὗτος ἐποίησεν καὶ τοὺς κρίκους τῆς σκηνῆς χρυσοῦς καὶ τοὺς κρίκους τῆς αὐλῆς καὶ κρίκους εἰς τὸ ἐκτείνειν τὸ κατακάλυμμα ἄνωθεν χαλκοῦς. Reference to ch. xxvi will show that the *golden* κρίκοι (hooks) were those used to join the two sets of tabernacle curtains (five in each set) together. The third set of κρίκοι mentioned in v. 19 are of copper and ought to be those which held the tent of goats'-hair curtains together (cf. xxvi. 11); for they were the only copper κρίκοι in the tabernacle.[1] With the second set, the κρίκοι τῆς αὐλῆς, it is difficult to decide whether the compiler intended to leave undesignated what metal they were made of, or whether he meant χαλκοῦς at the end of the verse to refer to them as well as to the third set. If he meant that they too were made of copper,

---

[1] Incidentally, their position in the list in v. 19 after the κρίκοι of the court possibly means that the compiler imagined the κατακάλυμμα here to be not the 'tent over the tabernacle' but the court-gate. If he did, he is wrong in stating its κρίκοι to be of copper, for they were of silver: cf. xxvii. 10 and 17, where κρίκοι and κεφαλίδες both represent וָו.

he is wrong, for these hooks for the court pillars were made of silver (see ch. xxvii). But however that may be, our immediate object is to compare these κρίκοι τῆς αὐλῆς of *v.* 19 with the ἀγκύλαι of *v.* 20. The latter says καὶ ἀγκύλας ἐποίησεν τοῖς στύλοις ἀργυρᾶς ἐπὶ τῶν στύλων, and immediately it becomes obvious that these silver ἀγκύλαι (hooks) are likewise the hooks for the court pillars. McNeile, p. 172, does suggest that these στῦλοι for which these silver ἀγκύλαι were made were the στῦλοι = קְרָשִׁים = frames, and he sees in this detail another evidence of a 'divergent tradition', since the M.T. knows nothing of silver hooks for the frames. But McNeile's suggestion is wrong, for a comparison of *v.* 20 with ch. xxxvii. 17, 18 shows that *v.* 20 almost certainly derived its information from ch. xxxvii. Chapter xxxvii. 17, 18 says of the pillars of the gate (πύλη) καὶ οἱ στῦλοι... καὶ ἀγκύλαι αὐτῶν ἀργυραῖ καὶ αἱ κεφαλίδες αὐτῶν περιηργυρωμέναι ἀργυρίῳ. καὶ αὐτοὶ περιηργυρωμένοι ἀργυρίῳ καὶ πάντες οἱ πάσσαλοι τῆς αὐλῆς κύκλῳ χαλκοῖ.

If the relevant parts of xxxviii. 20, 21 are immediately compared, the extensive similarity becomes very evident: both passages are referring to the hooks of the *court-* and *gate-*pillars... τῇ πύλῃ τῆς αὐλῆς· καὶ ἀγκύλας ἐποίησεν τοῖς στύλοις ἀργυρᾶς ἐπὶ τῶν στύλων. οὗτος περιηργύρωσεν αὐτούς (A-text). οὗτος ἐποίησεν καὶ τοὺς πασσάλους τῆς σκηνῆς καὶ τοὺς πασσάλους τῆς αὐλῆς χαλκοῦς.

Clearly the ἀγκύλαι mentioned by both these passages are the same, namely, the hooks for the court pillars. But the ἀγκύλαι in xxxvii. 17 represent the Hebrew וָוֵי (xxxviii. 19), and, of course, are the very same things as ch. xxvii calls κρίκοι (וָוִים) in its *v.* 10 and κεφαλίδες (וָוֵי) in its *v.* 27, and ch. xxxix. 6 (xxxviii. 28) calls ἀγκύλαι. This being so τοὺς κρίκους τῆς αὐλῆς of xxxviii. 19 and ἀγκύλας... τοῖς στύλοις ἀργυρᾶς of xxxviii. 20 are the very same objects, the hooks (וָוִים) of the court pillars.[1] It means that the compiler of these two verses has, without realizing it, duplicated his information; that he

---

[1] It might be argued that *v.* 20 describes the hooks on the gate pillars only and not the hooks on the rest of the court pillars; but the distinction, if intended, is not valid, since the Hebrew word is the same for all the hooks, and the seeming difference caused by the varying translations in the Greek is not a real one.

was not following any Hebrew, else he would not have made the mistake; and that for his information he drew upon both ch. xxvii and ch. xxxvii of the Greek. Now the varying translations of וָוִים in chs. xxvii and xxxvii do not, as we have seen, by themselves imply difference of translator; but the unintelligent combination of their variations in ch. xxxviii. 19 and 20 does seem to suggest that this section of ch. xxxviii, at least, is by a different hand. And this confirms the conclusions we drew from the repetition in *v.* 18 of the overlaying of the veil-pillars (already mentioned in xxxvii. 4) and from the mistaken statement in *v.* 18 that the στῦλοι (=frames) were 'covered with silver'.

3. THE CONFLICTING USAGES OF THE TERM ΚΕΦΑΛΙΣ

But before proceeding further, we must return to the contradiction between chs. xxxvii and xxxviii regarding the κεφαλίδες (see xxxviii. 20). It will be observed that if only κεφαλίδας in xxxviii. 20 could be taken to mean 'bases', the contradiction between the two chapters would disappear, for the information in xxxviii. 20 would then be correct: silver bases for the tabernacle, copper bases for the door and gate, the bases being of solid metal. At first sight such a meaning for κεφαλίδας seems impossible. κεφαλίς can, according to Liddell and Scott, mean an 'extremity', and even a 'foot' of a table; but a pillar has two extremities and the κεφαλίς ought to be the capital. And yet in xxxix. 4, 5 (xxxviii. 27) the Greek says τὴν χώνευσιν τῶν κεφαλίδων τῆς σκηνῆς καὶ εἰς τὰς κεφαλίδας τοῦ καταπετάσματος, ἑκατὸν κεφαλίδες εἰς τὰ ἑκατὸν τάλαντα, τάλαντον τῇ κεφαλίδι (A-text); but the Hebrew is talking of אֲדָנִים, 'bases'! Now in xxxviii. 20, because the Greek is not based on any (known) Hebrew, it is impossible to say what Hebrew word its κεφαλίδας is meant to represent; but here in xxxix. 4, 5 (xxxviii. 27) it is beyond doubt that κεφαλίδες is intended to represent אֲדָנִים. It is equally clear, however, that in spite of the meaning of the Hebrew word, κεφαλίδες is intended to have its proper meaning 'capitals', for in *v.* 6 (xxxviii. 28) it is used to represent רָאשִׁים, the Hebrew word for 'capitals'. Moreover, when ch. xxxix wishes to speak of 'bases', it calls them βάσεις, *vv.* 8, 9 (xxxviii. 30, 31); and it is impossible to think that the translator intended both κεφαλίδες and βάσεις, within the compass of six verses, to mean 'bases'. Admittedly we are then faced with this remarkable feat of translation:

$$vv.\ 4,\ 5\ \text{κεφαλίδες} = \text{אֲדָנִים}$$
$$v.\ 6\ \text{κεφαλίδες} = \text{רָאשֵׁיהֶם}$$
$$vv.\ 8,\ 9\ \text{βάσεις} = \text{אֲדָנִים}$$

but we have learned to recognize such inconsistent translation of technical terms as the normal style of the Greek version. Some will protest that the Hebrew must have changed since the translation was made and that the apparent inconsistency is due to this change. But the plea breaks down in face of an utterly stupid mistake on the part of the Greek in *v.* 6. From *v.* 2 onwards, the Greek, like the Hebrew (xxxviii. 25 f.), sets out to tell us how the *silver* offering was used. It accounts for the hundred talents, and then in *v.* 6 attempts to tell us what happened to the remaining 1775 shekels. It says ἐποίησαν εἰς τὰς ἀγκύλας τοῖς στύλοις καὶ κατεχρύσωσεν[1] τὰς κεφαλίδας αὐτῶν καὶ κατεκόσμησεν αὐτούς! This mistake cannot be charged on any change in the Hebrew, which simply says 'He made hooks for the pillars, and overlaid their capitals and filleted them'. The fact is, the translator is condemned out of his own mouth. He purports to tell us what happened to the 100 talents 1775 shekels of *silver* (*v.* 2) and then in a moment of absent-mindedness says that the 1775 shekels were used to overlay the capitals... with gold!! Evidence of his embarrassment is his translation κατεκόσμησεν for חִשַּׁק. The latter is the normal Hebrew for filleting and the normal translation in the second section is περιαργυρόω; but since the translator had gratuitously introduced gold, he had to depart from custom and translate חִשַּׁק κατεκόσμησεν. The translator, then, cannot be relieved of the charge that he has handled his Hebrew carelessly; but apart from this blunder, his use of the other technical terms, κεφαλίδες and βάσεις, appears to make good sense within its own context, provided only it is

---

[1] It might be argued that the change from third plural to third singular indicated that κατεχρύσωσεν was meant to begin a new sentence, having nothing to do with the silver shekels. But this cannot be so. Verse 6 of the Greek is clearly intended as a translation of the whole sentence xxxviii. 28 in the M.T. The change in the Greek may be a scribal error, even though a minority only (M(mg) fi egj b l) read the singular ἐποίησεν.

not compared with the Hebrew which it is meant to translate. It is just here that a major difference between ch. xxxviii and ch. xxxix in the use of κεφαλίδες comes to light. Ch. xxxix appears to speak of 100 silver capitals in the tabernacle (that is the tabernacle-building, not in the court) and so adds a detail nowhere mentioned before. But it does not thereby contradict anything in the first or second sections of the Greek. Ch. xxxviii, on the other hand, cannot avoid falling out with either ch. xxxvii or ch. xxxix. If by its κεφαλίδες it means 'capitals' (v. 20), then its copper capitals for the door and gate contradict ch. xxxvii and chs. xxvi and xxvii. If, however, to reconcile its information with that given in chs. xxvi, xxvii and xxxvii, its κεφαλίδες are interpreted to be 'bases', then its usage of κεφαλίδες is opposed to the usage of ch. xxxix; for the latter uses κεφαλίδες for 'capitals', and distinctly calls the copper bases of the door and gate βάσεις and not κεφαλίδες (xxxix. 8, 9). Moreover the remark in xxxviii. 18 that he covered the στύλους (=frames) with silver likewise conflicts with ch. xxxix; in giving account of the uses to which the silver was put ch. xxxix, like the Hebrew (xxxviii. 25f.), makes no mention of the frames being covered with silver.

To complete our investigation along this line, we must just consider the use of κεφαλίδες in ch. xl. The Hebrew in its v. 18 of this chapter describes the erection of the tabernacle, giving the details in their natural order: 'And Moses reared up the tabernacle, and laid its bases, and set up the frames thereof, and put in the bars thereof, and reared up its pillars.' The Greek has (xl. 16) καὶ ἔστησεν Μ. τὴν σκηνὴν καὶ ἐπέθηκεν τὰς κεφαλίδας καὶ διενέβαλεν τοὺς μοχλοὺς καὶ ἔστησεν τοὺς στύλους. It will be observed that the Greek is one phrase short, and we are left to decide whether its ἐπέθηκεν τὰς κεφαλίδας represents וַיִּתֵּן אֶת־אֲדָנָיו or וַיָּשֶׂם אֶת־קְרָשָׁיו. Hatch and Redpath choose the latter alternative, so making κεφαλίδας represent קְרָשִׁים; but they are almost certainly wrong, for

(1) κεφαλίδες in ch. xxxix = אֲדָנִים, though it is intended to mean 'capitals';

(2) ἐπέθηκεν, in this context, means 'to put on top' and makes tolerable sense 'he erected the tabernacle and put on its capitals'; whereas if κεφαλίδας referred to the frames, the Greek—'he erected the tabernacle and *put on* its frames'—would not make sense, since

the Greek has not mentioned any bases on which the frames could be put;

(3) קְרָשִׁים is everywhere else in Exodus represented by στῦλοι, but because the עַמּוּדִים are likewise translated στῦλοι the second section normally omits all reference to στῦλοι = קְרָשִׁים. The mention of στῦλοι = קְרָשִׁים in xxxviii. 18 is, as we have seen, unwitting and mistaken.

We may be confident, therefore, that κεφαλίδες in xl. 16 is used to represent אֲדָנִים. It is admittedly a mistranslation, but it is consistent with the usage of ch. xxxix and involves no contradiction of any other chapter in the Greek. In fact, leaving aside ch. xxxviii, we may say that κεφαλίδες always means 'capitals' in Exodus, though, in the normal style of the translator, it stands for various Hebrew words.

4. CONCLUSIONS

We come, then, to the conclusion that *vv.* 18–20, at least, of ch. xxxviii are by a different hand from chs. xxxvii, xxxix and xl; and the likelihood is that these verses are not based directly on any Hebrew, but are an incomplete compilation of details collected inefficiently from the Greek of the other chapters of Exodus.

But the claim that *vv.* 18–20 of ch. xxxviii are not based on any Hebrew is a sweeping one and needs to be substantiated. Each of the three verses begins with an (unnecessarily) emphatic οὗτος and so they are marked off from the preceding verses of the chapter, where each item is introduced by a plain καὶ ἐποίησεν. At the same time they are linked to the following verses of the chapter by the repeated use of this emphatic οὗτος; and the following verses can most definitely be traced to a Hebrew text in spite of their abbreviations and unauthorized additions. Now *vv.* 18–20 are plainly intended as a summary of metalwork, and so one might be inclined to suppose[1] that while there may never have been any Hebrew text which presented these details together as the Greek does, yet the Greek is founded on fragments of verses scattered here and there in the Hebrew text. The idea may be easily tested. If these verses are a direct translation from Hebrew, it ought to be easy to retrans-

[1] As Finn does, p. 468.

late them into reasonable Hebrew. In actual fact, if one does attempt it, one meets with considerable difficulties.

First, the κρίκοι (τῆς αὐλῆς) of *v.* 19 and the ἀγκύλας of *v.* 20 will both appear in Hebrew as וָוִים; and even if the Greek of *vv.* 19 and 20 was compiled from different Hebrew passages, וָוִים would each time occur in a similar context, namely the description of the court pillars, and would refer to exactly the same things. Now the translator of the first section rendered וָוִים variously by κρίκοι and κεφαλίδες; but he did it for the sake of deliberate variety. The situation is different in xxxviii. 18–20. This is meant to be a list and κρίκοι and ἀγκύλαι are obviously intended as different things. It is almost unthinkable that any translator, faced with the וָוִים in two similar contexts, should include them twice in one list under different translations. But if, as suggested above, the compiler drew his information from the Greek of chs. xxvii and xxxvii, it is quite understandable that in all innocence he should take κρίκοι and ἀγκύλαι as referring to different things and so include both separately in his list.

Another, and still bigger, difficulty will be how to retranslate κεφαλίδας in *v.* 20. It cannot be taken to represent וָוִים as in some parts of the first section, for κρίκους and ἀγκύλας stand here for וָוִים. Of the two remaining possibilities one would be to give κεφαλίδας its natural meaning, 'capitals', and to retranslate it by רָאשִׁים. This, as we have seen, would make xxxviii. 20 violently conflict with the Greek of ch. xxxvii and of the first section and with the M.T. everywhere. At the same time it would reduce the account given in xxxviii. 20 to absurdity. Later xxxviii. 20 says οὗτος περιηργύρωσεν αὐτούς,[1] he overlaid them (= the pillars) with silver; and of course the pillars referred to are the pillars of the court and court-gate (not the στῦλοι of *v.* 18 which are said to have gold, not silver, ἀγκύλαι). Give κεφαλίδας the meaning 'capitals' and we get this strange result: gate pillars, encased in silver, with solid silver hooks and yet with plain copper capitals! This is ludicrous. Again the passage tells us that the pillars of the door had copper 'capitals', but it tells us no more about these pillars. The veil

---

[1] This is the majority text. αὐτάς read by Bahnr is manifestly wrong: αὐτάς would refer to the ἀγκύλας which are said to be of solid silver. They would thus not need to be silver-plated.

pillars it says were overlaid with gold (*v.* 18), the gate pillars with silver (*v.* 20); it is disappointing that it does not tell us with what metal the door pillars were covered. They could scarcely have been left bare when the gate pillars were covered with silver; but again it would be ludicrous to have these pillars covered with silver or gold and their ornamental capitals to be of plain copper. But if these pillars were covered with metal, why is not the metal mentioned in this list, which clearly intends to be a summary of metalwork? This list is unsatisfactory to say the least; but it is altogether impossible to think that there ever was a Hebrew account that agreed with these Greek verses and had רָאשִׁים where they have κεφαλίδας.

The other possibility would be to suppose that κεφαλίδας stood for אֲדָנִים. אֲדָנִים means 'bases' and no one would ever have dreamed of supposing that κεφαλίδας could represent אֲדָנִים, did not chs. xxxix and xl, as we have seen, use κεφαλίδας in this way. Such usage is in fact so remarkable that it could only be explained if both xxxviii. 20 and ch. xxxix were by the same translator, or if the translator of one passage had borrowed from the other.

Now it is clear that in ch. xxxix κεφαλίδες does not *mean* 'bases' although it stands for אֲדָנִים; it has its natural meaning, 'capitals'. When ch. xxxix wishes to speak of 'bases', it calls them βάσεις (*vv.* 8, 9). But if we suppose that κεφαλίδας in xxxviii. 20 stands for אֲדָנִים, it becomes impossible to find any suitable meaning for κεφαλίδας. It cannot mean 'capitals' as in ch. xxxix, unless we are prepared to accept the absurd consequences detailed above. The meaning 'bases' would make the information of xxxviii. 20 agree with ch. xxxvii and the first section; but it is utterly impossible to think that any translator should commit such an outrage against language as to use κεφαλίδας to *mean* 'bases', when its natural meaning in a context like this is the very opposite.

Next, if κεφαλίδας cannot *mean* 'bases', we search the list of metalwork in xxxviii. 18–20 and find that it has no reference to any bases whatsoever. This is strange. The bases were of solid cast copper and silver (just as *v.* 20 wrongly says the κεφαλίδας were) and one would have expected that, in a list of metalwork, the bases would certainly be mentioned above all else. Once more we notice that this list is incomplete and unsatisfactory;

but the absence of any mention of bases, and the fact that, if κεφαλίδας could only *mean* bases, it would banish every difficulty and make xxxviii. 20 agree with the story as given in the M.T., begin to point clearly to the solution of the problem.

Meanwhile it will help us if we make one further observation on the use of κεφαλίδες in ch. xxxix. 4 (xxxviii. 27). κεφαλίδες here stands for אֲדָנִים (bases). These bases were for the frames and veil pillars, and were of solid cast silver, weighing a talent each. Each frame had two bases, and the purpose in having such heavy bases was of course to keep the frames standing up straight. The translator of xxxix. 4 has taken it upon him to render אֲדָנִים by κεφαλίδες which he intends in the sense of capitals. In doing so he shows a serious lack of perception, for now his frames have no bases to support them, while each has at its top two talents of solid silver which would make it exceedingly difficult to keep the frames standing up at all. According to the M.T. the frames and veil pillars had no capitals: but even the door and court pillars, which had capitals, had those capitals overlaid with metal, not made of solid metal. It is idle to suppose a Hebrew text which had the silly story which we find here in the Greek, when the whole difficulty manifestly springs from a mistranslation. This mistranslation, however, is in ch. xxxix confined to the אֲדָנִים of the frames and veil pillars; the אֲדָנִים of the door, court and gate pillars are properly rendered βάσεις. In xxxviii. 20 the mistranslation is generalized for the אֲדָנִים of the door and gate as well, and it is this generalization that produces most of the nonsense.

All these difficulties, then, point to the same conclusion. The original mistranslation, κεφαλίδες, was made by the translator of ch. xxxix. Chapter xxxviii. 18–20 is a very carelessly compiled and incomplete list that has culled its information not directly from a Hebrew text, but indirectly and with obvious lack of understanding from the Greek of other chapters.[1] In particular it has taken the translation κεφαλίδες of ch. xxxix and, without realizing what lay behind it, has unwittingly extended it until it makes nonsense that cannot be reconciled with the surrounding Greek, but is readily explained as soon as one consults the Hebrew underlying the original mistranslation in ch. xxxix.

But the mere presence of this list in the Greek translation calls

[1] For further evidence on this point, see Appendix II, p. 114.

for some explanation, since, as remarked above, the Greek is nowhere given to unnecessary repetition. The evidence suggests strongly that the list is not by the same hand as translated chs. xxxvii and xxxix. Who then compiled the list, and how did it get into all the Greek MSS., and why does it stand in this curious position between the record of the making of the tabernacle furniture and the making of the court furniture?[1] These questions must be deferred until we come to consider the bigger problem of the Greek order of the whole second section. There it will appear that not only is xxxviii. 18–20 in a curious position, but so too is the whole of ch. xxxviii.

[1] Finn, p. 476, notices the curious position of this list in relation to its context and has an ingenious theory to account for it.

CHAPTER VII

FURTHER PECULIARITIES OF CHAPTER XXXVIII

WE have already noticed the differences and discrepancies between ch. xxxviii. 18–20 and the rest of the Greek Exodus. Apart from these verses, ch. xxxviii records the making of all the tabernacle furniture except the golden altar. The differences between its account and the corresponding parts of the first section of the book are many; some of them are extreme.

We will take first the account of the making of the copper altar. Says *v.* 22, 'He made the copper altar out of the copper censers which belonged to the men who rebelled with the company of Korah'. Not a word of this appears anywhere in the Hebrew of Exodus, or in the Greek of ch. xxvii. The story of Korah's rebellion and the censers is in the Hebrew related in Numbers. McNeile, p. 233, infers that the story in Numbers contradicts Exod. xxvii. He says 'According to Num. xvi. 36–40 (xvii. 1–5) the bronze covering of the altar was made at a later time. And in the LXX of the present passage (Exod. xxxviii. 22) there is an attempt to harmonize the accounts.' It is not so, however; neither the Hebrew nor the Greek of Numbers implies that the altar was made only of bare wood until the rebels' censers provided some copper to cover it. The copper censers were evidently used as an additional covering, as the Greek of Numbers says 'προσέθηκαν αὐτὰ περίθεμα τῷ θυσιαστηρίῳ'. The two accounts, then, do not need harmonizing. Moreover, if they did, the Greek of Exod. xxxviii would make a very poor job of it. It merely says 'He made the copper altar out of the copper censers'. There is no mention of the wooden framework, and so it does not harmonize with Exod. xxvii. At the same time it is not a true account of the story given in Numbers to say 'he *made* the altar out of the censers'. So, then, Exod. xxxviii. 22 is a very ill-digested piece of information agreeing neither with Exod. xxvii nor with the story in Numbers. But it is interesting to see that xxxix. 10 (xxxviii. 30) has been edited to make it agree with xxxviii. 22. The Hebrew says that among the things made from the copper-offering were the copper altar and its copper grate. The Greek has the grate but omits the altar, because according to xxxviii. 22 the altar itself was not made from the copper-offering. Now we have already proved that part of ch. xxxviii is not by the same hand as chs. xxxvii and xxxix. It is probable, therefore, that this attempt to make ch. xxxix agree with ch. xxxviii was deliberate editing done in the course of compiling ch. xxxviii in its present form. That there has been such editing done, and done with such a motive, is an important piece of evidence to remember.

Continuing its account of the altar ch. xxxviii says in *v.* 23 (read the A-text) τὴν βάσιν αὐτοῦ καὶ τὸ πυρεῖον αὐτοῦ καὶ τὰς φιάλας καὶ τὰς κρεάγρας. The Hebrew (xxxviii. 3) has אֶת־הַסִּירֹת וְאֶת־הַיָּעִים וְאֶת־הַמִּזְרָקֹת אֶת־הַמִּזְלָגֹת וְאֶת־הַמַּחְתֹּת. φιάλας and κρεάγρας are the well-recognized equivalents for מִזְרָקֹת and מִזְלָגֹת; but βάσιν probably results from a misreading of the Hebrew. The βάσις of the altar is יְסוֹד in Hebrew; the word used here is סִירֹת and means 'pots'. The Hebrew words are quite similar and might easily get confused. Strangely enough the translator of the corresponding verse in the first section likewise, it seems, misread סִירֹת. His equivalent στεφάνη (crown) (xxvii. 3) is at first sight so far removed from the Hebrew סירתיו that *B.H.* suggests that the LXX read זֵר לַמִּזְבֵּחַ (a crown to the altar), while others have thought that the LXX was following a different Hebrew tradition in which the copper altar had a crown just as the ark, table and golden altar had. But in xxv. 23, 25 (xxv. 27) στεφάνη is used for מִסְגֶּרֶת and it is very probable that in xxvii. 3 סירתיו was misread as מסגרת. If so, it is interesting that both xxvii. 3 and xxxviii. 23 have made a mistake over the same term, but not the same mistake.

But to return to the list of vessels as given in xxxviii. 23. If we are right in taking βάσιν as the (mistaken) equivalent for סִירֹת (the B-text has a different order), it means that יָעִים has no Greek equivalent; for πυρεῖον, if it has its normal meaning, must, though out of order in the list, represent מַחְתֹּת. Here again it is interesting to see that the translator of xxvii. 3 likewise ran into difficulties over יָעִים. He found at the beginning of his list סִירֹתָיו לְדַשְּׁנוֹ וְיָעָיו. The first two Hebrew terms go together, 'its pans to take away its ashes', while יָעָיו means 'its shovels' with which they put the ashes into the pans. The Greek, as we have already observed (p. 53), mistook the first term, and in consequence ran into trouble with the next two. All that stands to represent them is τὸν καλυπτῆρα αὐτοῦ; and since this is a thoroughgoing mistake, it is difficult to know whether it is meant to be a combined translation of the two terms or whether יָעָיו has been ignored altogether. It is not a little curious, then, that xxxviii. 23 has no translation for יָעָיו; for we have previously discovered that the compiler of ch. xxxviii is dependent for some of his information on the Greek of the earlier chapters.

Now it scarcely needs to be repeated that the Greek of ch. xxxviii calls the grate of the altar τὸ παράθεμα, 'the appendage', which is a widely different translation from ἡ ἐσχάρα, 'the hearth', of ch. xxvii. The use of the word πυρεῖον in ch. xxxviii, however, needs further examination. In v. 23 πυρεῖον seems to be used normally for מַחְתָּה, but in v. 24 it is used again. The grate is said by the Hebrew to be under the ledge (כַּרְכֹּב) that encircled the altar; the Greek has it κάτωθεν τοῦ πυρείου. If, then, πυρεῖον in this verse is intended in a different sense from πυρεῖον in the previous verse, the translator must have been utterly careless to introduce such confusion. If he intended it in the same sense as in v. 23, it is evident that he had not the slightest notion what the πυρεῖον of v. 23 was. It is a strange thing that מַחְתֹּת, 'firepans', should be translated in the singular, τὸ πυρεῖον, in both ch. xxvii and ch. xxxviii. Whether the translator of ch. xxvii failed to understand what the מַחְתֹּת were is difficult to say. The position of πυρεῖον in the list in xxxviii. 23, and the fact that the Greek has four terms instead of the Hebrew's five, again make it doubtful whether the translator of ch. xxxviii knew to what Hebrew word πυρεῖον referred. The Hebrew word כַּרְכֹּב, which πυρεῖον in v. 24 represents, occurs only in Exod. xxviii and xxxviii. It is evident that the translator of ch. xxvii had trouble with it: he renders it by ἐσχάρα, seemingly misreading it for מִכְבָּר which also he translates ἐσχάρα. Perhaps, then, we are justified in thinking that πυρεῖον in xxxviii. 24 is a mistranslation due to ignorance. At any rate, our general conclusions must be that while both Greek accounts of the altar show signs of incompetence, the second is the worse; it is not following the Hebrew closely; its additional information is ill digested and incorrectly stated; and it is altogether so different from the first account as to make it practically certain that it is not by the same translator as ch. xxvii.

The description of the ark in ch. xxxviii is heavily abbreviated and paraphrased. The making of its staves, for instance, is mentioned, not in its proper place, but along with the making of the staves for the table (*v.* 11). The account of the table is likewise much abbreviated, and repeats the mistake of ch. xxv in saying that the table was made of pure gold, and omitting all reference to its wooden frame. Again, the ark, table and copper altar were all carried by staves which were put through rings on their sides. The rings are described by the Hebrew as 'places for the staves', בָּתִּים לַבַּדִּים. For this ch. xxxviii has the strange translations εὑρεῖς τοῖς διωστῆρσιν (*vv.* 4 and 10), εὑρεῖς τοῖς μοχλοῖς (*v.* 24). The translations of בָּתִּים in this connection in the first section are all different; εἰς θήκας xxv. 25 (27), εἰς οὓς εἰσάξεις xxvi. 29 and ψαλίδες xxx. 4; but they are all reasonable translations. The use of εὑρεῖς for בָּתִּים is confined to ch. xxxviii—naturally, for בָּתִּים in this sense does not occur elsewhere in chs. xxxv–xl. But how did the translator get εὑρεῖς out of בָּתִּים? In the Aramaic of Dan. iii. 1 there occurs the word פְּתָי (+suffix). In the pre-Theodotion 'θ' text[1] it is translated εὖρος. Is it possible that the translator of Exod. xxxviii mistook בתים for some form of פתי or פתה? (The Aramaic פתה = to be spacious.) At any rate, however he arrived at the translation, it is manifestly different in style from the renderings used in chs. xxv–xxxi; and, whereas they differ each time, εὑρεῖς is employed consistently in ch. xxxviii.

When we come to the description of the lampstand in xxxviii. 13–17, we find that the differences, especially in the technical terms, between this account and the one in ch. xxv are more than with any other part of the tabernacle. Certain things are at once evident: like the account of the ark and table, the description of the lampstand is much abbreviated. At the same time it has additions explaining the position and purpose of some of the details, for instance *v.* 16 ἅ ἐστιν ἐπὶ τῶν ἄκρων and again τὰ ἐνθέμια...ἵνα ὦσιν ἐπ᾽ αὐτῶν οἱ λύχνοι. This is strongly reminiscent of the Targums; the Targum of Palestine, for instance, attempts in Exod. xxvii and xxxviii an explanation of the purpose of the grate of the copper altar. It raises the

[1] See Ziegler, *Daniel*, Göttingen (1954), pp. 61f.

question whether the translator is paraphrasing the Hebrew text that we now have, or whether he has abandoned that, and is following a Targumic text. Perhaps we shall never know; but it is at least evident that the lampstand he endeavours to describe is the same in its general features as the lampstand described in ch. xxv. In that chapter *v.* 30 (31) the lampstand has five components: ὁ καῦλος, οἱ καλαμίσκοι, οἱ κρατῆρες, οἱ σφαιρωτῆρες, τὰ κρίνα. Likewise in ch. xxxviii. 13–17 it has five components: ὁ καῦλος, οἱ καλαμίσκοι, οἱ βλαστοί, τὰ λαμπάδια, τὰ ἐνθέμια. The first two are the same, the other three are different. Now ch. xxv interprets the Hebrew to mean that there are three κρατῆρες but only one σφαιρωτήρ and one κρίνον in each branch. So also ch. xxxviii has it that there are three βλαστοί in each branch, but only one λαμπάδιον and one ἐνθέμιον; for the λαμπάδια are said to be on the ends of the branches (ἐπὶ τῶν ἄκρων) while the seventh ἐνθέμιον is ἐπ' ἄκρου τοῦ λαμπαδίου ἐπὶ κορυφῆς ἄνωθεν, that is, on top of the central shaft, and that leaves one ἐνθέμιον for each of the six branches.

So far, then, the two accounts agree, although they use different terms. But here the real differences begin. The βλαστοί ought from their number to correspond to the κρατῆρες; but while ch. xxv says (rightly according to its Hebrew) that the κρατῆρες were ἐκτετυπωμένοι καρυΐσκους it is not the βλαστοί but the λαμπάδια that were καρυωτά according to ch. xxxviii. Yet if on that account we try to equate the κρατῆρες with the λαμπάδια we run into further difficulties. λαμπάδια is an itacism for λαμπαδεῖα[1] and in Zech. iv. 2, 3 the large bowl of the lampstand is called λαμπαδεῖον. But this bowl was the receptacle of the main oil supply and quite a different thing from the bowls which Exod. xxv calls κρατῆρες. The Hebrew terms, too, are of course different: גֻּלָּה for the λαμπαδεῖον and גְּבִיעַם for the κρατῆρες. Possibly λαμπαδεῖον is intended to have a different sense in Exod. xxv from what it has in Zech. iv, for the situation is further complicated by the fact that while in Zech. iv גֻּלָּה is represented by λαμπαδεῖον, in Eccl. xii. 6 it is rendered ἀνθέμιον: and as Grabe long ago observed, ἐνθέμιον in Exod. xxxviii. 16 is a corruption of ἀνθέμιον. But again

[1] See P. Katz, *Theol. Zeitschr.* v (1949), p. 5 = *Actes du premier Congrès de la Fédération Internationale des Associations d'Etudes Classiques* (Paris, 1951), p. 168.

ἀνθέμιον in Exodus is more likely because of its literal meaning to represent פֶּרַח (flower) and McNeile says, p. 167 note, that in the Mishna the word פֶּרַח is employed to denote the *tray* of a lamp. Yet elsewhere פֶּרַח has other equivalents: in III Kingd. vii. 35 (49) λαμπάδια is used for פֶּרַח, while in Num. xvii. 8 (xvii. 23)—the account of Aaron's rod that budded—פֶּרַח is translated by βλαστός, a term that ch. xxxviii of Exodus also employs for the lampstand (*v.* 15). The only conclusion that one can come to is that in the Septuagint the terms relating to lampstands are inextricably confused.

In the midst then of such a welter of inconsistency, it is probably idle to attempt to reconcile the terms of ch. xxv with those of ch. xxxviii. The account in ch. xxv is a straightforward translation of its Hebrew and its terms fairly represent their Hebrew counterparts. The ch. xxxviii account is a paraphrase, and, because of the general laxity in the use of technical terms, it is impossible to say with certainty what Hebrew words lie behind its description.

The chapter concludes with the account of the making of the laver (*vv.* 26, 27). It was made from the mirrors of the women who served (LXX 'fasted': does this come from reading צוּם for צָבָא?)[1] at the door of the tent of meeting. The Greek has felt a difficulty: how could they fast at that door, when, at the time when they gave their mirrors, the tabernacle was not yet erected? So it adds its own explanatory note: they fasted 'on the day he pitched it'—that is, the tabernacle. Then it has another addition giving the purpose of the laver (*v.* 27): 'And he made the laver, that Moses and Aaron and his sons might wash their hands and feet thereat, when they went into the tabernacle of testimony; or whenever they came near to the altar to minister, they washed thereat, as the Lord commanded Moses.' The source of this addition is not far to seek. The addition is a very slightly modified translation of ch. xl. 31, 32 (Heb.). When we turn to ch. xl in the Greek, we find it lacks completely these verses describing the place and purpose of the laver. We can only conclude that they have been removed to ch. xxxviii by the compiler of that chapter; and we are not surprised, for we have already noticed how ch. xxxix has been edited to make it agree

[1] L. Cappellus, cf. Schleusner (1820), vol. IV, p. 16, and P. Katz, *Philo's Bible*, p. 149.

with the ch. xxxviii account of the copper altar. This is further evidence that ch. xxxviii is dependent, not on a different Hebrew text, but on the Greek of other chapters of Exodus.

Some, nevertheless, will be inclined to think that the Greek order is original here, that is, that the Heb. xl. 31, 32, which is doubtless the source of the Gk. xxxviii. 27, once stood in a Hebrew text immediately after the account of the making of the laver. A moment's investigation shows it cannot be so. The Heb. xl. 17–33 gives the account of the erection of the tabernacle and the positioning of the furniture. The Gk. xl. 15–27 attempts to translate this account, but its omissions are such that if the Greek account is in fact the original one, then on the great day when the tabernacle was erected,[1] they

(1) spread out the tabernacle and tent curtains with no frames (στῦλοι = קְרָשִׁים) to support them (vv. 16, 17);
(2) put no mercy-seat on the ark (v. 18);
(3) put no screen at the door;
(4) put no screen at the gate; and
(5) had no laver at all: for it is to be noticed that the Greek not only puts the description of the function of the laver in ch. xxxviii instead of here, but it completely omits here all mention of the laver.

The incompleteness and absurdity of this account show that it is not original.

Moreover in the M.T. account, as each piece of furniture is mentioned, its purpose and function are described, thus:

xl. 22, 23, table: he set the bread in order upon it.
xl. 24, 25, lampstand: he lighted the lamps.

---

[1] For the purposes of this argument it does not matter whether there ever was an actual tabernacle erected. It is here a question of judging these accounts as pieces of literature and not, for the moment, as historical records. The notion that a coherent, sensible and consistently detailed account can only be the result of many attempts and many recensions is grotesque. When archaeologists find shattered fragments of pottery which on being pieced together form two-thirds of a symmetrical vase, they suppose that the vase was originally complete and restore the lost third accordingly. So with the Hebrew and Greek of Exod. xl. The Hebrew is a perfectly symmetrical composition; the Greek reproduces that symmetry in part, but with evident gaps. And even these gaps can be largely filled with pieces from ch. xxxviii (Gk.) which have no known Hebrew authority for standing in their present context. Obviously the Hebrew account is the original; the Greek is a broken and dislocated copy.

xl. 26, 27, golden altar: he burnt incense thereon.

xl. 29, altar of burnt-offering: offered upon it the burnt-offering and meal-offering.

xl. 30–2, laver: to wash withal.

The Greek translation gives the purpose and function of the first three pieces of furniture; mentions the altar of burnt-offering without giving its function, and entirely omits the laver. The very inconsistency of the Greek account tells against its being original. And when we see that the Greek has a translation of the Hebrew verses that give the function of the laver, but that it puts this translation in ch. xxxviii, it becomes very evident that the Greek has removed these verses from their original and proper context.

Perhaps the biggest difference between ch. xxxviii and the first section of Exodus is its omission of all reference to the making of the golden altar; it has been held by scholars to be extremely significant. We shall, however, postpone discussing it to a later chapter. Meanwhile we must begin to draw together the evidence so far collected. Our last chapter demonstrated that while variations in the translation of technical terms are insufficient to prove that the second section is by a different translator from the first, some part of ch. xxxviii is not homogeneous with the other chapters of the second section: it contradicts them so thoroughly that it must be regarded as the work of another hand. The present chapter, by its examination of the further peculiarities of ch. xxxviii, has shown that the whole chapter is completely different from the first section and is either by a different translator from the first section, or else has been much altered by a later editor.

CHAPTER VIII

THE EVIDENCE OF NUMBERS

THE whole weight of probability has thus far been in favour of the view that the second section of Exodus, apart from ch. xxxviii, is by the same translator as the first section. This view is further strengthened—only slightly, perhaps, but appreciably neverthe-less—by a consideration of the Greek of Numbers. The trans-lation of this book has mistakes in common with the Greek of both first and second sections of Exodus.

We noticed in Ch. VII how the translator of Exod. xxvii. 3 ran into difficulties with the list of utensils belonging to the copper altar. He misread סִירֹתָיו and translated it στεφάνην and for the next two terms לְדַשְּׁנוּ וְיָעָיו he put only one τὸν καλυ-πτῆρα. He is thus convicted of a bad mistake, for the first two Hebrew terms go together, 'its pans to take away its ashes', while יָעָיו means 'its shovels' with which they put the ashes into the pans (p. 53). Now in Num. iv. 13 the command וְדִשְּׁנוּ אֶת־הַמִּזְבֵּחַ is translated καὶ τὸν καλυπτῆρα ἐπι-θήσει ἐπὶ τὸ θυσιαστήριον. Obviously this rendering has some-thing in common with Exod. xxvii. 3; yet if this were all, it might be argued that the translators of Exodus and Numbers were, independently of each other, following a traditional, but mistaken, interpretation of the verb דִשֵּׁן. But this is not all. In the next verse in Numbers a list of utensils is given: τὰ πυρεῖα καὶ τὰς κρεάγρας καὶ τὰς φιάλας καὶ τὸν καλυπτῆρα. The Hebrew has אֶת־הַמַּחְתֹּת אֶת־הַמִּזְלָגֹת וְאֶת־הַיָּעִים וְאֶת־הַמִּזְרָקֹת. The last two terms in the Greek are thus shown to be out of order, for φιάλας is the normal translation not of יָעִים but of מִזְרָקֹת. This means that τὸν καλυπτῆρα stands for יָעִים. So then Numbers uses καλυπτήρ both for דִשֵּׁן and for יָעִים. This is remarkable and requires some explanation. Such inconsistency in the rendering of technical terms is, of course, quite in the style of Exodus and Leviticus. But that Exod. xxvii. 3 should render לְדַשְּׁנוּ וְיָעָיו by καλυπτῆρα, and that Numbers should render וְדִשְּׁנוּ by καλυπτῆρα ἐπιθήσει (iv. 13) and הַיָּעִים by καλυπτῆρα (iv. 14), cannot be regarded as a mere coincidence. It could be understood if (1) Numbers and Exodus first section were by the same translator, or (2) Numbers were dependent on Exodus for its rendering here.

It is evident that translators elsewhere in the O.T. found יָעִים a difficult word: in III Kingd. vii. 26 and 31 (40 and 45) it is twice translated θερμάστρεις, but in IV Kingd. xxv. 14 the translator contents himself with an attempt at transliteration, τὰ ιαμιν.[1] It might be, therefore, that the translator of Numbers likewise found it difficult and turned for help to Exod. xxvii. 3. There he found the one phrase τὸν καλυπτῆρα αὐτοῦ for the two Hebrew terms לְדַשְּׁנוֹ וְיָעָיו, and in consequence used καλυπτήρ himself indiscriminately both for the verb דִּשֵּׁן and the noun יָעִים.[2]

Either supposition, of course, implies that the first section of Exodus was translated before Numbers.

[1] The spelling with μ, ιαμιν, may well be corrupt.

[2] 'This is a fresh example to illustrate a strange aspect of septuagintal translation Greek. Here it is due to inadequate knowledge of Hebrew and lack of exegetical tradition, which makes a translator look out for guidance from earlier translations. Similarly κώδων "bell" as a translation of רִמּוֹן "pomegranate" II Par. iv. 13 can be understood only from the translator's superficial look at Exod. xxviii. 33 f., where he found, side by side and closer than in the Hebrew, ῥοΐσκους=רִמּוֹנִים "pomegranates" and κώδωνας =פַּעֲמוֹנֵי "bells" and picked out the wrong one. Other instances, however, are not due to careless borrowing. One of them is pentateuchal. As Deissmann has observed (Bible Studies, pp. 100 ff.) ἄφεσις stands for יוֹבֵל ten times in Lev. xxv. 28–54, five times in Lev. xxvii. 17–24, and in Num. xxxvi. 4. The reason for this obviously inadequate rendering is easily found in Lev. xxv. 10–13. Here ἄφεσις 10a correctly renders דְּרוֹר, but the same translator interprets יוֹבֵל הוּא 10b–12 by the composite expression (ἐνιαυτὸς) ἀφέσεως σημασία αὔτη, בִּשְׁנַת הַיּוֹבֵל חַזֹּאת 13 by ἐν τῷ ἔτει τῆς ἀφέσεως σημασίᾳ αὐτῆς (σημασίᾳ αὐτῃ Ahy). This conglomeration he considered a unit to such a degree that he managed to use one of its components, ἄφεσις, for the whole of it. The same explanation applies to the unintelligible rendering Πολυανδρεῖον of גַּיְא "valley, chasm" in Jer. xix. 2, 6 and ii. 23. Here the development can be observed in Ezekiel: in xxxix. 12 (11b), 15, 16 גַּיְא הֲמוֹן גּוֹג is literally rendered τὸ Γαι τὸ Πολυανδρεῖον τοῦ Γωγ, with גַּיְא transliterated and הֲמוֹן ably translated. Since, however, גֵּי הָעֹבְרִים xxxix. 11a is rendered τὸ Πολυανδρεῖον τῶν ἐπελθόντων, we must presume that the translator employed Γαι and Πολυανδρεῖον synonymously (along with φάραγξ 11c and elsewhere) and thus was able to use the latter for גַּיְא instead of repeating his transliteration. Admittedly this explanation implies that the Greek of Jer. xix and Jer. ii. 23 is influenced by the Greek Ezekiel.

But there is also evidence to suggest that the translator of Numbers is dependent on the Greek of the second section of Exodus. In the Hebrew of Num. iii. 36 and again in iv. 31 there occurs the phrase קַרְשֵׁי הַמִּשְׁכָּן וּבְרִיחָיו וְעַמֻּדָיו וַאֲדָנָיו. The Greek has each time τὰς κεφαλίδας τῆς σκηνῆς καὶ τοὺς μοχλοὺς αὐτῆς καὶ τοὺς στύλους αὐτῆς καὶ τὰς βάσεις αὐτῆς. Here there can be no doubt that κεφαλίδας represents קַרְשֵׁי while the אֲדָנִים are properly translated βάσεις. But κεφαλίδες as a translation of קְרָשִׁים is outrageous. Where can it have come from? On p. 46 we observed that the account of the erection of the tabernacle, Exod. xl. 16 (18), is one phrase short in the Greek; and we were left to decide whether its ἐπέθηκεν τὰς κεφαλίδας represented וַיִּתֵּן אֶת־אֲדָנָיו or וַיָּשֶׂם אֶת־קְרָשָׁיו. For the reasons there given we chose the former alternative. Hatch and Redpath, however, choose the latter and so make κεφαλίδες represent קְרָשִׁים. It is probable then that the translator of Numbers did likewise. He may well have consulted the last chapter of Exodus—the easiest chapter in a scroll to consult—and decided that κεφαλίδες was the proper equivalent for קְרָשִׁים. Had he turned to earlier chapters he would have found that the Greek of Exodus has no separate equivalent for the קְרָשִׁים. Where it mentions them it uses στῦλοι as for the עַמֻּדִים; but very often it does not trouble to mention them separately at all (p. 74).

If, then, this suggestion is right, the translator of Numbers is dependent on the mistaken Greek of the second section of Exodus for his translations in chs. iii and iv. But in this same ch. iv he has, as has been shown, much in common with the Greek of the first section of Exodus; and this must mean that the Greek of both sections of Exodus (apart from ch. xxxviii) was in existence when Numbers was translated.

Now it is noticeable that some of the terms which Numbers uses to describe the lampstand in its chs. iv and viii agree with Exod. xxxviii against Exod. xxv. It has, for example, (viii. 4) στερεά for מִקְשָׁה instead of τορ⟨ν⟩ευτή; (iv. 9) λαβίδες for מֶלְקָחַיִם instead of ἐπαρυστῆρες; (iv. 9) ἐπαρυστρίς for מַחְתָּה instead of ὑπόθεμα. Common usage of ordinary terms such as

Certainly the Greek of Jer. xix differs strikingly from the normal Greek of the parallel passage in Jer. vii; some even suggest that in the Hebrew much of Jer. xix is not original.' P. Katz

these, however, does not have the same significance as agreement in mistakes and unusual translations such as we have considered above. It does not prove that Numbers is dependent
on Exod. xxxviii; if there were any dependence at all, it could
as easily be that Exod. xxxviii is following Numbers. But there
need have been no dependence at all; both could be independently following the same tradition. Moreover Num. viii. 4
uses κρίνον for פֶּרַח in the manner of Exod. xxv. So then, while
the relation of Numbers to Exodus seems to suggest that the
bulk of both sections of the Greek Exodus was already in
existence when Numbers was translated, there is nothing to dis-
prove our tentative conclusion that Exod. xxxviii in its present
state is later than the rest of the book.

CHAPTER IX

CONTENTS OF THE GREEK
SECOND SECTION

WE set out in Ch. v to examine the problem of the second section of Exodus by investigating its use of technical terms. We must now face the question of its contents. To measure these contents, we shall compare the Greek with the M.T. The M.T., of course, is thus used only for sake of convenience; it does not imply that the M.T. is necessarily the correct standard by which any deviation in the Greek is shown to be secondary. To guard the reader against such a misunderstanding we shall not speak of 'additions' and 'omissions' in the Greek, unless and until the Greek is proved to be secondary. Where the Greek contains something that is not in the M.T. we shall call it a 'plus', and where the Greek lacks something that is in the M.T. we shall call it a 'minus'.

Then we must consider not only the 'pluses' and 'minuses' in the Greek, but also its proportions. Sometimes the Greek cannot be said to lack a certain article, but its account of that article is so short that the Greek passage lacks a good deal of information that appears in the M.T.

We shall recognize at once, of course, that many minor 'pluses' and 'minuses' are caused by nothing more than the common accidents of textual transmission (which tend to be numerous in passages full of technical detail) and the influence of similar, frequently repeated, phrases elsewhere in Exodus and the rest of the Pentateuch. Our task is not with these[1] but with the larger 'pluses' and 'minuses' that seem to indicate a serious difference between the Greek and the M.T.

I. 'PLUSES'

The 'pluses' are as follows:

(1) Ch. xxxv. 19: the anointing oil and the incense.

(2) Ch. xxxviii. 16: certain phrases explaining the purpose of some of the parts of the lampstand.

[1] Finn, p. 461, gives a list of them.

(3) Ch. xxxviii. 22: explanation of the source of the copper for the copper altar.

(4) Ch. xxxviii. 26: time note: 'on the day when he pitched it'.[1]

(5) Ch. xxxix. 12: the sentence: 'And of the remaining gold of the offering they made vessels with which to minister before the Lord.'

The list of metalwork in xxxviii. 18–20 and the verse giving the purpose of the laver, xxxviii. 27, appear at first sight to be 'pluses'; but we have already seen (p. 47) that the list is a compilation of information drawn from other parts of the Greek, while xxxviii. 27 has been transposed from ch. xl where it originally represented the Hebrew *vv.* 31, 32 (see p. 57). They are not therefore 'pluses' in the strict sense at all.

We are left then with the five 'pluses' listed above, and we notice that three of them come in ch. xxxviii. They have already been discussed (pp. 52–7) and there is no need to repeat the conclusion that, while they constitute real differences between the Greek and the M.T., the chapter in which they occur is not in its present state the work of the original translator of the rest of the second section.

The 'plus' in xxxv. 19 about the anointing oil and incense, when it is compared with the context, is seen to be altogether superfluous and out of place. It comes at the end of a list (xxxv. 9–19) in which both items have already been mentioned (*v.* 14).[2] Certainly both mentions of the anointing oil and incense would not have stood in the original translation nor presumably would any subsequent editor have knowingly duplicated the information. The addition is most likely an early accident in the textual transmission; such accidents are quite common, especially in lists of technical details like these. Moreover, seeing drastic abbreviation is the marked style of the translator in the second section, we may not even suppose that he translated his Hebrew list completely in all its detail. And

---

[1] At first sight the addition in xl. 15 (17) 'in the second year *after they came out of Egypt*' appears to resemble this one. But really they are different. In xl. 15 the Greek merely makes an explanatory addition, based on other parts of Exodus, to a time note already in our Hebrew; in ch. xxxviii. 26 it adds a time note for which it has no known authority.

[2] Finn, p. 461, points out the significant fact that the corresponding list in ch. xxxi. 6–11 has these items at the end.

since it is possible to detect in the MSS. more than one subsequent attempt to complete the list, the resultant confusion in content and order makes the list very difficult to use as evidence for the Hebrew text which the original translator employed.

The 'plus' in xxxix. 12 about 'the remaining gold' has no known authority. At first sight it seems a suitable neighbour to *v.* 13 which speaks of 'the remaining blue, purple and scarlet'; but when we come to examine the detailed order of this passage (see p. 88) we shall find that *v.* 12 is really out of place in its present context. Its resemblance to *v.* 13 is only superficial. It may therefore be a part of the original translation that has become displaced, or it may be a later editorial insertion: we have no means of deciding. And this 'plus' is the only really important one outside ch. xxxviii.

2. 'MINUSES'

A large part of the Hebrew of the second section does not appear in the Greek. Much of this disparity is accounted for by the policy of wholesale abbreviation which the translator deliberately adopted; it is without any great significance. The serious disagreements are those where the Greek seems to lack completely the account of certain major items. Foremost among these is the total absence from the Greek of any record of the making of the incense altar. It has been thought to be highly significant, and to prove that the Greek of the second section followed a Hebrew tradition that knew nothing of an altar of incense. But the conclusion was hasty, for the Greek lacks other things as well, the goats'-hair curtains for instance, and the skins and the frames; and it would be difficult to argue a like significance for these 'minuses'. Presumably no Hebrew tradition ever envisaged an arrangement such as the Gk. ch. xxxvii gives: a tabernacle formed of ten curtains without protective coverings; in which the dividing veil is supported on four pillars (*v.* 4), the door on five (*v.* 5), and yet the ten large curtains themselves have no supports whatever! Obviously the 'minuses' must be examined more carefully before conclusions are drawn.

The incense altar

The first thing to notice is that it is ch. xxxviii which is responsible for the absence of the golden altar; and only when it has been discovered who compiled ch. xxxviii in its present state, with all its mistakes and absurdities, will it be safe to argue anything from the absence of the incense altar.

Then, as Finn has pointed out (p. 476), the place of this altar in ch. xxxviii is taken by that strange list of metalwork that we have already examined (pp. 41 f.). Whatever we may think of Finn's suggested explanation,[1] the list's being in this position can scarcely be a coincidence. The list itself we have concluded (p. 47) was not compiled by the original translator, but it may well have been inserted by an editor to fill in a gap. At the same time the Origenic MSS. appear to indicate that Origen's *Vorlage* did contain an abbreviated notice of the making of the incense altar, so that it may quite possibly be that our non-Origenic MSS. have accidentally lost an original οὖτος ἐποίησεν τὸ θυσιαστήριον τὸ χρυσοῦν.[2]

Again it is not true to say that the second section as a whole lacks the incense altar. Chapter xl. 5 mentions it quite clearly and so does ch. xl. 24 (26). Now ch. xl agrees fairly closely with the M.T. throughout. Some will say therefore that ch. xl is a late addition in the Greek and on that account includes the incense altar. But ch. xl of the Greek everywhere lacks the laver, and the theory that regards the inclusion of the incense altar as 'late' also contends that the absence of the laver is 'early'.[3] Evidently this theory does not explain the state of the Greek text of ch. xl, nor is any such theory needed here. Chapter xl as we have seen (pp. 57–9) once had in its second half (after *v.* 26) an account of the laver (answering to the Heb. xl. 30–2) which was subsequently removed to ch. xxxviii. The absence of the laver from the first half of ch. xl (it should come in *vv.* 6 and 10) probably results therefore either from the translator's abbreviation or from an accident in the transmission. To argue that the first part of ch. xl is early because it contains no laver, and the second part late because it once contained the laver, would be absurd. The second part lacks the mercy-seat[4] (it should come

[1] 'that for some reason, such as the mutilation of a page, the text used by the translators was here defective, and that they therefore filled up the gap by stringing together the fragments about the metal-work from other parts'.

[2] For a full discussion of this point see p. 113.

[3] Cf. McNeile, pp. 195, 198.

[4] This involves the omission of one phrase out of five that describe things done to the ark. The omission may easily have been caused by parablepsis.

in *v.* 18, Heb. xl. 20), though ch. xxv of both Hebrew and Greek describes it. Both parts also lack the screen for the court-gate, and this surely has no weighty significance.

But to return to the incense altar. The list in xxxv. 9–19 (Heb. xxxv. 10–19) does lack this altar and so, apparently, does the list in xxxix. 14–21 (Heb. xxxix. 33–41). These lists, however, show evident signs of confusion in the Greek. The order of articles, for instance, in the first list is:

> the tabernacle...the ark of the testimony and its staves and its mercy-seat, and the veil, and the curtains of the court and its pillars, and the emerald stones and the incense and the anointing oil, and the table and all its vessels and the lampstand of light and all its vessels and the altar and all its vessels and the holy robes of Aaron the priest and the robes in which they shall minister, and the garments for the sons of Aaron for priestly ministry and the anointing oil and the compound incense.

We have already noticed (p. 65) that this list repeats the anointing oil and incense, but still more remarkable is the position it gives to the hangings for the court and its pillars. They come between the ark and the table—just where in fact we might expect to find the incense altar—and are immediately followed by the emerald stones which have nothing to do with the context, and by the anointing oil and incense which are well in place (in the Hebrew (xxxv. 15) they follow the incense altar). There can be no reasonable doubt that the Greek list has suffered dislocation; and when it is seen that the court hangings are not only out of place but come exactly where the incense altar should be, one cannot help thinking that some accident or else some inept editing is responsible for the omission of this altar from the list, and the insertion of the court hangings in their present position.

The list in xxxix. 14–21 (xxxix. 33–41) likewise shows some disturbance, but specially interesting is the order of the furniture: 'the ark...the altar and all its vessels, and the anointing oil and the compound incense and the pure lampstand...and the table...'. The altar mentioned here would seem from its position to be the incense altar, for though it is not stated to be the golden altar, it is mentioned along with the interior furniture, where the copper altar would be quite out of place. It is, moreover, followed most appropriately by the anointing oil and incense. On the other hand, this list has no reference to the copper altar, if *v.* 16 refers to the golden altar. It does seem, therefore, that there has been some confusion here over the two altars; for the altar of *v.* 16 is not said to be golden and the phrase 'and all its vessels' has no Hebrew authority, if the altar is meant to be the incense altar, whereas in the Hebrew the copper altar *is* accompanied by that phrase.

It is not then a case of plain, straightforward 'absence' of the golden altar. The matter is confused; and before we decide upon the cause of this confusion it will be well to consider the other 'minuses'.

The laver

Apart from ch. xxxviii, there is now no mention of the laver any-where in the Greek second section. The position is thus the reverse of what it is with the incense altar which is missing from ch. xxxviii but is mentioned elsewhere in the second section. We have already seen (pp. 57–9) that ch. xl once contained an account of the laver somewhere about *v.* 26. To correspond with the M.T. it ought to mention the laver in its *v.* 6 (Heb. *v.* 7) and again in its *v.* 10 (Heb. *v.* 11). The absence of the laver from these two verses is all the more striking because the Greek of ch. xl is (for Exodus) very close to the M.T., which makes it less likely that the Greek is following a tradition that lacked the laver.[1] The first mention of the laver should come after the altar of burnt-offering in *v.* 6. It is perhaps significant that, after the place where the laver should come, the Greek text once more shows signs of confusion. The M.T. after the laver has (*v.* 8) 'And thou shalt set up the court round about, and hang up the screen of the gate of the court'. Vaticanus B and its allies read καὶ περιθήσεις τὴν σκηνὴν καὶ πάντα τὰ αὐτῆς ἁγιάσεις κύκλῳ. Here σκηνήν is obviously wrong, and the correct αὐλήν is read by AFM and their allies. These MSS. likewise omit the mistaken καὶ πάντα τὰ αὐτῆς ἁγιάσεις so that κύκλῳ immediately follows αὐλήν as it should. But they still have no mention of the hanging of the gate-screen: in other words they lack some such sentence as: καὶ ἐπίθησεις τὸ κάλυμμα τῆς πύλης τῆς αὐλῆς. This omission may result from nothing more than parablepsis (αὐλήν...αὐλῆς) just as the phrase καὶ πάντα τὰ αὐτῆς ἁγιάσεις

---

[1] I.e. less likely than if the lack had occurred in a chapter like ch. xxxviii.

read by B etc. seems to be an intrusion based on v. 9.[1] It may be that the absence of the laver too was originally caused by some such textual accident. Yet it is not a little curious that the Greek subsequently lacks the laver again (in v. 10) and the gate-screen (in v. 27, Heb. v. 33). This surely cannot be a coincidence; but if these 'minuses' are deliberate, it means that any explanation of them that can only explain the absence of the laver but not of the gate-screen is unsatisfactory.

Now when we search the rest of the second section for references to the gate-screen, we find this striking fact. Chapter xxxvii follows the M.T. very closely in all that it chooses to translate, just as does ch. xl. Yet while it lacks any reference to the tent (= the eleven goats'-hair curtains) and the frames—two big structural items—it has six verses, xxxvii. 13–18 (Heb. xxxviii. 15–20) giving in full the account of the gate and its screen! Contrarily ch. xl mentions the goats'-hair curtains which ch. xxxvii omits! The M.T. of ch. xl. 19 says: 'And he spread the tent (= the eleven goats'-hair curtains) over the tabernacle (= the ten linen curtains) and put the covering (= the two sets of skins) of the tent upon it.' This the Greek xl. 17 renders fully (even if it uses the terms unintelligently): καὶ ἐξέτεινεν τὰς αὐλαίας ἐπὶ τὴν σκηνὴν καὶ ἐπέθηκεν τὸ κατακάλυμμα τῆς σκηνῆς ἐπ' αὐτῆς ἄνωθεν. Here τὰς αὐλαίας[2] are the goats'-hair curtains, while, confusingly enough, σκηνή refers first to the linen curtains (מִשְׁכָּן) and then to the goats'-hair curtains (אֹהֶל). It shows, of course, that the translator did not fully understand his technical terms, but it shows all the more that he was blindly following a text identical here with the M.T.

Any absence of the gate-screen, laver and goats'-hair curtains is therefore most easily accounted for as the result of abbreviation on the part of the original translator, made worse, maybe, by subsequent accident in the transmission. To attempt to

---

[1] Rahlfs takes the opposite view that B's reading is all original. But this would mean that the translator (or his *Vorlage*) had unnecessarily duplicated some of the information regarding the hallowing of the tabernacle. Moreover until v. 9 there has been no reference to the anointing oil, so that the announcement in v. 9 'And thou shalt take the anointing oil...and hallow it (the tabernacle)...' looks like the intended start of the hallowing section.

[2] There is no need to think as *B.H.* suggests that the Greek read הַיְרִיעֹת or הַקְּלָעִים. We know too much about the translator's way with technical terms for that.

account for the presence or absence of these three things alone in chs. xxxvii, xxxviii and xl on the theory of earlier and later Hebrew recensions involves so many contradictions as to reduce the theory to absurdity.

But to return to the question of the laver. There are two other places in the second section where we should expect the laver to be mentioned but where in fact it is absent. They are the two lists which we have already partly discussed (p. 68), xxxv. 9–19 (xxxv. 10–19) and xxxix. 14–21 (xxxix. 33–41). In the first list the M.T. has the laver in this position: '...the altar of burnt-offering, with its grating of copper, its staves, and all its vessels, the laver and its base, the hangings of the court, the pillars thereof, and their sockets, and the screen for the gate of the court'. We have already seen (p. 68) that in the Greek 'the hangings of the court and the pillars thereof' have been moved from their natural position and placed among the interior furniture. And since the hangings of the court are the items that should come immediately after the laver, this dislocation in the Greek list may well account for the absence of the laver. Again, the Hebrew adds to the major pieces of furniture their subsidiary vessels thus: (*v.* 13) the table and its staves and all its vessels and the shewbread; (*v.* 14) the lampstand also for the light, and its vessels, and its lamps and the oil for the light; (*v.* 16) the altar of burnt-offering with its grating of copper, its staves and all its vessels; (*v.* 17) the hangings of the court, the pillars thereof and their bases and the screen for the gate of the court.

The Greek consistently abbreviates: (*v.* 15) the table and all its vessels; (*v.* 16) the lampstand of light and all its vessels; (*v.* 17) the altar and all its vessels; (*v.* 12) the hangings of the court and its pillars. It is quite possible that the translator mistook the laver and its base as vessels subsidiary to the altar and did not trouble to translate them separately. But whatever the cause it is important to notice that the problem here is to account for the absence from the list, not merely of the laver (and incense altar), but also of the following articles: the frames and tabernacle-bases, staves of the table and shewbread, lamps and oil for the light, the screen for the door, the altar's copper grating and its staves, court-bases, screen for court-gate, the pins of the tabernacle and the pins of the court and their cords. Was there ever a Hebrew tradition that knew nothing of all these things?

The list in xxxviii. 14–21 (xxxix. 33–41) is remarkable most of all for its order; the Greek shows signs of having been deliberately altered according to a definite scheme. The question of order, however, must be left till our next chapter. For the moment we may observe that when the Greek order is disentangled, the Greek is found to follow the M.T. quite closely (see pp. 94–8). It is far less abbreviated than the list in ch. xxxv, and yet in addition to its confusion over the two altars (see pp. 68–9) it lacks the tabernacle-clasps and frames and the mercy-seat.[1] In the M.T. the laver and its base follow as usual immediately upon 'the copper altar and its copper grating, its staves and all its vessels'. In the Greek the only mention of an altar comes, as we have seen (p. 68), between the ark, and the anointing oil, incense and lampstand. The altar is not described as either golden or copper, no mention of a grate is made either here or anywhere else in the list,[2] and its staves are left out. In fact all we get is the vague: 'and the altar and all its vessels'. Its position in the list suggests it is the golden altar, but the phrase 'and all its vessels' is found in the M.T. with the copper altar only. It is probable therefore that (1) originally the phrase 'the altar and all its vessels' referred in the Greek to the copper altar and that the laver and its base were included by the translator as adjuncts to the altar, or (2) that the 'laver and its base' were accidentally dropped out when the confusion arose over the two altars and/or when the Greek list was changed to its present order (p. 97).

The goats'-hair curtains

Chapter xxxvii contains a brief notice of the making of the ten linen tabernacle curtains. It gives two short verses (1, 2) to what in the M.T. occupies six verses (xxxvi. 8–13). But it lacks completely the making of the eleven goats'-hair curtains and the two sets of skin coverings (Heb. xxxvi. 14–19). Scholars have not commented so much on this 'minus', but it would be equally as important as the absence of the incense altar and laver if it could be taken as evidence that the Greek was following a

---

[1] The absence of the mercy-seat may have been caused by parablepsis after the Greek list had been changed to its present order, thus: καὶ τὸ ἱλαστήριον καὶ τὸ θυσιαστήριον.

[2] The mention of the copper grate in v. 10 belongs to another, quite distinct, list.

Hebrew text that did not contain an account of the goats'-hair curtains. The fact is, however, that no such deduction can be made from this 'minus', for the Greek mentions these curtains in several other places in this section. In xxxv. 6 it has τρίχας αἰγείας, in xxxv. 10 (11) τὰ παραρρύματα = אֶת־אָהֳלוֹ = its tent.[1] In xl. 17 (19) τὰς αὐλαίας clearly stands for אֶת־הָאֹהֶל, as we have already seen (p. 70); but in xxxix. 14 (33) the position is more confused. The Hebrew here begins a list of the tabernacle articles as they were brought on their completion to Moses: 'They brought the tabernacle (= the ten linen curtains) . . . the tent (= the eleven goats'-hair curtains) and all the instruments thereof, the clasps thereof (which fastened the curtains together), the frames thereof (over which the curtains were spread), the bars thereof (which kept the frames together) . . . .' The Hebrew order is natural and its use of technical terms precise. The Greek list begins 'τὰς στολὰς . . . τὴν σκηνὴν καὶ τὰ σκεύη αὐτῆς . . .'. Something is obviously wrong with στολάς, for even if it were the original translation, the mention of στολάς here would be out of place. Popper, indeed, maintains, pp. 160–3, that στολάς is a deliberate rendering of another Hebrew text, and represents the cloths that covered the sacred vessels on the march; but it is an impossible explanation. For any text, Hebrew or Greek, to mention such cloths first in this list along with the big structural components of the building would be absurdly inappropriate.[2] It is far easier to take τὰς στολὰς and τὴν σκηνήν as standing simply but mistakenly for מִשְׁכָּן and אֹהֶל. If the mistake is the work of the original translator, it is no worse than the many other mistakes which we have already found in both the first and second sections. The mistake could also be the result of unintelligent editing or even scribal error, for στολάς occurs nearby in the previous verse (13).

So then the Greek of the second section, in spite of its lack in ch. xxxvii, followed a Hebrew text which like the M.T. did contain many references to the goats'-hair curtains. Admittedly

---

[1] 'The tent' is the technical term for the eleven goats'-hair curtains.

[2] For further discussion of this point see pp. 89–90. *B.H.* suggests that the Greek represents a Hebrew text which had 'tabernacle-cloths and tent'. But there is no need to project on to 'a Hebrew text' the inept mistranslations and mistakes of the Greek.

the Greek does not translate the technical term, אֹהֶל, consistently; but all this demonstrates is that the second section shows the same attitude towards technical terms as the first section.

Similarly the skins, absent from the Greek ch. xxxvii, are nevertheless mentioned in xxxv. 7, xxxv. 10 (11) (τὰ κατακαλύμματα = מִכְסֵהוּ = its covering = the skins), xxxix. 21 (34), and xl. 17 (19) (κατακάλυμμα).

The frames

The most complete and consistent 'minus' in the second section is the absence of the frames (στῦλοι = קְרָשִׁים). No account of their making is given in ch. xxxvii and they are absent from the lists in xxxv. 10 (11), xxxix. 14 (33) and xl. 16 (18). The sole reference to them in this section is in xxxviii. 18, and there, as we have seen (pp. 41f.), the reference is unwitting and results from a misreading of the Greek of the first section.

Now it would be difficult to think that this 'minus' was caused by a Hebrew *Vorlage* that knew nothing of frames, since no alternative means of supporting the tabernacle curtains are mentioned. Actually the Greek gives fairly clear evidence that its Hebrew *Vorlage* must have mentioned the frames, for the Greek constantly speaks of the bars (μοχλοί = בְּרִיחִים) which held the frames together, xxxv. 10 (11), xxxix. 14 (33) and xl. 16 (18), and without the frames the bars are useless. Similarly the Greek mentions the bases (βάσεις = אֲדָנִים) in xxxix. 14 (33) and again in xxxix. 4 (xxxviii. 27) and xl. 16 (18), though in these two passages κεφαλίδες and not βάσεις is used for אֲדָנִים;[1] and without the frames there would be nothing to stand in these bases.

We do better, therefore, to look in the Greek itself for the cause of the 'minus'. The first section (see p. 20) uses στῦλοι for both frames and pillars of the veil, door, court and gate. The second section in ch. xxxvii gives a full account of the στῦλοι for the veil, door, court and gate, but lacks the στῦλοι = frames and the bars and bases that went with these στῦλοι. In its lists, however, the second section mentions bases, bars and στῦλοι

[1] Note that in xxxix. 4 (xxxviii. 27) the 'κεφαλίδων τῆς σκηνῆς' are clearly distinguished from the 'κεφ. τοῦ καταπετάσματος', and must be the κεφ. belonging to the frames.

thus: xxxv. 10 (11) bars and στύλους, xxxix. 14 (33) bases, bars and στύλους, xl. 16 (18) bases (κεφαλίδας), bars and στύλους. It is evident from their position that the στῦλοι each time are the pillars and not the frames; but since the bases and the bars are mentioned it is perhaps possible that στῦλοι = frames has been accidentally omitted from the lists. In xl. 16 (18), on the other hand, the omission involves not one word only, but a whole phrase answering to the Hebrew 'and he set up the frames', and it would be a very strange coincidence if this phrase and all the other references to the στῦλοι = frames had been *accidentally* omitted. The omission is surely deliberate; the original translator, or some subsequent editor, has omitted or removed all reference to the frames, but has left, somewhat unintelligently, the references to the bars and bases. And it would seem that this omission must have been earlier than the inclusion in xxxviii. 18 of the unwitting mention of στῦλοι = frames. The motive for this and for the other omissions that have been considered will be studied later (pp.76f.); for the moment we must turn to the matter of proportions.

3. PROPORTIONS

It has often been stressed that while ch. xxxvi gives a full translation of the making of the priests' vestments, the remaining chapters of the second section have a more or less abbreviated rendering of the tabernacle. Some have thought that this indicates that the Greek was following a Hebrew text that in this way showed its special interest in the priests' vestments. If that were so, how could the proportions of ch. xxxvii (Heb. xxxvi. 8, 9, 35–8, xxxviii. 9–23) be interpreted? Chapter xxxvii gives an extremely abbreviated account of the ten linen tabernacle curtains—two verses compared with the M.T.'s six—lacks altogether the goats'-hair curtains, the skins and the frames, and yet its account of the veil and veil pillars, door and door pillars, court, gate and their pillars with the bases, capitals, hooks and pins, is quite full and corresponds very closely with the M.T. What special interest does that evince?

Popper, on the other hand, suggests (see p. 6 above) that ch. xxxvi is original LXX and thus is translated as fully as the first section; but that chs. xxxvii–xxxix. 13 are not original

75

LXX, and this accounts for their abbreviations, paraphrases and Targumic additions. This view overlooks three things:

(1) It is ch. xxxviii only which has Targumic additions; additions elsewhere in the second section are practically insignificant.

(2) Abbreviation and paraphrase are not peculiar to the second section. The first section takes similar liberties (see Ch. IV). It abbreviates, omits and, in one instance (see p. 25), adds unauthorized details that make nonsense of the directions for the court-gate. If then there is any difference between the first and second sections in the matter of abbreviations, omissions and paraphrase, it is in degree only and not in kind.

(3) In spite of 'minuses' and abbreviations, chs. xxxvii–xl demonstrably follow a text that corresponds very closely with the M.T.[1]—not so closely of course as the first section does, but far more closely than has sometimes been realized.

Moreover we may now add that even the big 'minuses' of incense altar, laver, goats'-hair curtains and frames do not imply that the translator's Hebrew *Vorlage* did not contain these things. The evidence rather suggests that his Hebrew did contain these things, and that means that the Hebrew behind chs. xxxvii, xxxix and xl was throughout practically the same as we have in the M.T.; and the 'minuses' are in fact omissions on the part of the Greek.

4. CONCLUSIONS

How then are we to account for this strange attitude on the part of the translator to his task, his text being sometimes translated fully, sometimes abbreviated, sometimes completely omitted, and that disproportionately and with no apparent plan or purpose? If these chapters are in large part by the translator of the first section, there is an immediate answer. He was, as we know, impatient of technical details and certainly careless of accuracy in translating technical terms. Having waded through all the technical details once (and that not without letting his impatience lead him into some foolish mistranslations), when he encountered these details again he would weary of them, and considering it pointless to have a full repetition, he would shorten his work by wholesale abbreviations, paraphrases and

[1] The reader can gather some idea of this by observing the Greek and Hebrew verse-numberings in B.M. for chs. xxxvii, xxxix and xl.

omissions.[1] At the same time his impatience would show itself in his lack of principle and proportion in his abbreviating and paraphrases. And if he very drastically abbreviated the account of the making of the furniture, it is understandable that someone later should have attempted to fill it in, with the result that we now find in ch. xxxviii. If, on the other hand, we are asked to think that chs. xxxv–xl, or even chs. xxxvii–xl, are by another translator who deliberately sat down to translate these chapters in order to fill in what was lacking in the original Septuagint, his performance is so haphazard and incomplete that it is impossible to imagine a translator who would intentionally perpetrate such an inefficiency.

It still remains to be explained, of course, why, if both sections are by the same translator, the second section follows such a widely different order from the M.T., when the first section follows the M.T.'s order strictly. In our next chapter we shall discover that the present order of the Greek is not original, and that the Greek once stood in the same order as the M.T. The editing responsible for the change to the present order was deliberate but somewhat unintelligent, and has left behind a certain amount of debris in the text. It may well be then that much of the confusion which we have noticed in the lists of chs. xxxv, xxxix and xl has sprung from the same cause. Finally we may well suppose that a certain amount of omission has been caused by early copyists' mistakes which are no longer traceable in the MS. evidence. A technical text full of small details falls an easy prey to these errors; but a text that has suffered as much rearrangement as ours has will inevitably have more than the normal quota of such accidents.

[1] Cf. the Greek translation of Job, which abbreviates heavily, at times even freely epitomizes (G. Gerleman, *Book of Job* (Lund, 1946), pp. 23f.), and yet occasionally indulges in unauthorized additions. See Swete, Introd. pp. 255f.

CHAPTER X

THE ORIGINAL ORDER OF
THE SECOND SECTION

THE differences between the Hebrew and Greek order of the subject-matter at the end of Exodus seem at first sight to be many and large. Actually there are only two major differences; but they are so very large that if we can find out the truth about them we shall probably have the answer to all the minor differences (that is, of course, those that are not the result of scribal error merely).

The two major differences concern, first, the position of the furniture. The M.T. puts the court hangings, gate and pillars *after* the furniture; the Greek puts them *before* the furniture, immediately after the tabernacle curtains, veils and pillars; second, the position of the vestments. The M.T. puts them in ch. xxxix, the Greek in ch. xxxvi.

Our task is to discover whether

(1) the Greek order is original, that is, it followed a Hebrew text that stood in this order and that disagreed with the M.T., whose general arrangement the Greek normally follows; or

(2) the Greek order is not original, that is, its Hebrew *Vorlage* stood in a different order from our present Greek, an order which either agreed with the M.T. or followed yet a third arrangement; and we must also find out whether the present Greek order is due to the whim of the translator, or the result of some subsequent re-arrangement.

I. THE POSITION OF THE FURNITURE

The account of the furniture (except the golden altar) is contained in the Greek in one chapter, namely, ch. xxxviii. In this, the Greek resembles the M.T. which assembles in one section, xxxvii. 1–xxxviii. 8, all the furniture (including the golden altar). Now when the immediate context of the Greek ch. xxxviii is closely examined, we find that

(1) the preceding verses, namely, xxxvii. 19–21, agree closely with the M.T. xxxviii. 21–3;

(2) the following verses, namely, xxxix. 1–9, agree closely with the M.T. xxxviii. 24–31.

That is to say ch. xxxviii interrupts, in the Greek, verses that correspond to a connected passage in the M.T. Moreover the Greek has been agreeing closely with the M.T. not only from xxxvii. 19 but from xxxvii. 7; and at the other end, after a few confused verses (xxxix. 10–13), the Greek again follows the general order of the M.T. to the end of the book. The situation may helpfully be expressed in tabular form thus:

Greek	M.T.
xxxvii. 7–18	equals xxxviii. 9–20
xxxvii. 19	xxxviii. 21
καὶ αὕτη ἡ σύνταξις τῆς σκηνῆς τοῦ μαρτυρίου καθὰ συνετάγη Μωυσῇ, τὴν λειτουργίαν εἶναι τῶν Λευιτῶν διὰ Ιθαμαρ τοῦ υἱοῦ Ααρων τοῦ ἱερέως.	This is the sum of the tabernacle, even the tabernacle of the testimony as it was counted according to the commandment of Moses, the service of the Levites, by the hand of Ithamar, the son of Aaron the priest.
xxxvii. 20	xxxviii. 22
καὶ Βεσελεηλ ὁ τοῦ Ουριου ἐκ φυλῆς Ιουδα ἐποίησεν καθὰ συνέταξεν Κύριος τῷ Μωυσῇ.	And Bezalel the son of Uri, the son of Hur, of the tribe of Judah, made all that the Lord commanded Moses.
xxxvii. 21	xxxviii. 23
καὶ Ελιαβ ὁ τοῦ Αχισαμακ ἐκ τῆς φυλῆς Δαν, ὃς ἠρχιτεκτόνησεν τὰ ὑφαντὰ καὶ τὰ ῥαφιδευτὰ καὶ ποικιλτικά, ὑφᾶναι τῷ κοκκίνῳ καὶ τῇ βύσσῳ.	And with him was Oholiab, the son of Ahisamach, of the tribe of Dan, an engraver and a cunning workman, and an embroiderer in blue, and in purple, and in scarlet and fine linen.
Ch. xxxviii	
xxxix. 1	xxxviii. 24
πᾶν τὸ χρυσίον ὃ κατειργάσθη....	All the gold that was used....

79

xxxix. 9

...τοὺς πασσάλους τῆς σκηνῆς, καὶ τοὺς πασσάλους τῆς
αὐλῆς κύκλῳ.

xxxviii. 31

...all the pins of the tabernacle and all the pins of the
court round about.

| Confused verses: xxxix. 10–13 | | xxxix. 1–32: Priests' vestments |

xxxix. 14–xl. 32 follows general order of xxxix. 33–xl. 38.

It will be seen that if ch. xxxviii (Gk.) is for the moment excised, harmony is restored between the Greek and the M.T. order from xxxvii. 7 to xxxix. 9 (Gk.). Now this Greek section (less ch. xxxviii) not only follows the same order as the M.T. but is (for an Exodus passage) quite close to the M.T. in its content and detail. Chapter xxxviii, on the other hand, is in this respect quite different from its surrounding Greek. Though it refers generally to the same objects as the M.T. it differs greatly from it in its detail (see Ch. vii). Moreover ch. xxxviii in several matters disagrees with its own Greek context, so that in its present form it must be regarded as the work of a later editor (see Ch. vi). We have discovered too (see pp. 41–50) that this editor was inefficient and was sometimes dependent on (a mis-understanding of) the earlier Greek.

These considerations, then, create a strong presumption that the present position of ch. xxxviii is not the plan of the original translator; and this presumption is confirmed by further investigation. For this we start again from the observation that if it were not for ch. xxxviii, the Greek xxxvii. 19–xxxix. 9 would exactly correspond to the M.T. xxxviii. 21–31. Now this passage in the M.T. is a logical whole and stands in a logical position with regard to its context. By the time the M.T. reaches xxxviii. 20 it has completed the record of the making of the tabernacle. Thereupon xxxviii. 21 remarks 'This is the sum of the tabernacle...', and there follow the names of the chief workmen, and a list of the materials used. There can be no doubt that this order is deliberately designed.

At the same time the present Greek order seems to be deliberate. Chapter xxxviii groups together the furniture. Its 'special portion', vv. 18–20 (there is no similar portion in the M.T. or in the Greek first section), is a list of metalwork. That being so, the way it divides into two separate parts this passage, that in the M.T. is a connected whole, is significant; for the verses that thus immediately *follow* ch. xxxviii, namely, xxxix. 1–9 (Heb. xxxviii. 24–31), form another list (namely, of the materials used). Then since the priests' vestments, which in the M.T. follow this list, stand in the Greek in ch. xxxvi, the Greek is here left only with what are virtually three more lists:

xxxix. 14–23 (xxxix. 33–43): a list of the completed articles brought to Moses.

xl. 1–14 (xl. 1–16): a list of the tabernacle articles with the directions to erect, position and anoint.

xl. 15–32 (xl. 17–38): a list of the tabernacle articles with the account of their erection.

This grouping together of lists is probably deliberate.

Again the verses that in the Greek immediately *precede* ch. xxxviii, namely, xxxvii. 19–21, give the names of the chief workmen. The last of them, Eliab, has his work specified in detail.[1] The Greek translation puts it that he was in charge of the weaving, sewing and embroidery work, to weave in scarlet and linen; and this may give us a clue to the understanding of the order of the Greek before ch. xxxviii. The two major differences from the M.T. order are just these: the Greek puts *before* ch. xxxviii (the account of the furniture) the priests' vestments (xxxvi. 8–40) and the court hangings, gate and pillars (xxxvii. 7–18); and both these groups involve Eliab's weaving, sewing and embroidery, with the mention of which the section before ch. xxxviii closes. These chs. xxxvi and xxxvii admittedly omit some of the soft fabrics, namely, the goats'-hair curtains and the skins, and, on the other hand, they include the pillars for the veil, door, court and gate with the capitals, bases and pins, which involve the use of wood and metal. They are not therefore exclusively a list of soft fabrics. Nevertheless it remains true, as Finn (p. 469) has pointed out, that everything involving the use of textiles—vestments, veil, door, court and gate—has been grouped together and placed before ch. xxxviii.

This Greek order, then, seems to be deliberate, and our suspicion is confirmed by the order of the Greek list, xxxix. 14–23 (xxxix. 33–43). In this list the M.T. puts the tabernacle

---

[1] Unlike Oholiab of whom it is merely said that he 'did as the Lord commanded Moses'—ἐποίησεν καθὰ συνέταξεν Κύριος τῷ Μωυσῇ.

(= the ten linen curtains), the tent (= the eleven linen curtains), the skin coverings and the veil at the beginning (*vv.* 33, 34); the door-screen after the incense altar and before the copper altar (*v.* 38); the court hangings and gate after the laver (*v.* 40); and the vestments at the end (*v.* 41). Its order is quite logical: it starts with the building and then lists the other things, working from the inside outwards. The Greek list starts with a mistaken στολάς (see p. 73) and subsequently shows signs of confusion (see p. 68); but its conclusion is remarkable. After the table of shewbread, it reads (*v.* 19) 'and the robes of the holy place, which belong to Aaron, and the robes of his sons for the priestly ministry and the hangings of the court and the pillars, and the veil of the door of the tabernacle and of the gate of the court, and all the vessels of the tabernacle and all its instruments, and the hides, rams' skins dyed red and the coverings of purple skins and the coverings of the remaining things, and the pins and all the instruments for the service of the tabernacle of testimony'. In other words at the end of this list the Greek has grouped all the soft fabrics (plus a few other details such as pillars, vessels and pins) just as it has in chs. xxxvi and xxxvii.

It appears, therefore, that not only is the Greek order on both sides of ch. xxxviii deliberate but ch. xxxviii, coming just where it does in its immediate context, is the king-pin in the whole arrangement. But if ch. xxxviii in its present form is, as we think it is, the work of a later editor, then it becomes practically certain that the present Greek order is not the work of the original translator.

Here, however, we must digress to consider the question from another—and in fact completely opposite—point of view. The M.T.'s statement in xxxviii. 21, 'This is the sum of the tabernacle', seems to be quite natural and intelligible. All the tabernacle articles have now been made and it is appropriate to follow on with a summary of the workmen and materials. The Greek translation, xxxvii. 19, has αὕτη ἡ σύνταξις τῆς σκηνῆς..., 'This is the *arrangement* of the tabernacle'. Now from what we know of the translator's method in Exodus, such a mistranslation (if it is a mistranslation) would strike us as nothing unusual. Popper, however, pp. 158–65, 201, maintains that σύνταξις is not a mistranslation, but an accurate rendering of the Hebrew term; and that moreover when we examine the

Hebrew term in the light of its correct Greek translation, we find the key to the problem of the order of the text: the Greek order represents the original Hebrew tradition, the M.T. order is secondary and mistaken. It will help us to understand Popper, if we first put the Hebrew text in full:

אֵלֶּה פְקוּדֵי הַמִּשְׁכָּן מִשְׁכַּן הָעֵדֻת אֲשֶׁר פֻּקַּד עַל־פִּי מֹשֶׁה עֲבֹדַת הַלְוִיִּם בְּיַד אִיתָמָר בֶּן־אַהֲרֹן הַכֹּהֵן: 'this is the sum(?) of the tabernacle, even the tabernacle of the testimony, as it was counted at the commandment of Moses, the service of the Levites by the hand of Ithamar, the son of Aaron the priest'.

Popper's argument turns on the meaning of אֵלֶּה פְקוּדֵי and עֲבֹדַת. He maintains that this עֲבֹדָה (service) which was 'under the supervision of Ithamar' was the same as that which is described in detail in Numbers, chs. iii and iv. There the three families of the tribe of Levi are assigned their particular tasks in the dismantling, carrying and erection of the tabernacle and Ithamar is set to supervise one section of the work (Num. iv. 28 and 33). Accordingly the phrase אֵלֶּה פְקוּדֵי in Exodus means, says Popper, not 'this is the sum' but 'this is the arrangement' in the sense of the apportioning of the several parts of the tabernacle to the care of the Levites. And giving the phrase this meaning he suggests that it was originally intended to refer not to the list of materials which now follows it in the M.T., but to the tabernacle articles which precede it. In other words the Hebrew xxxviii. 21 originally meant that all the articles previously described came under the supervision of Ithamar. Popper then examines the present order of the M.T. in the light of this interpretation and concludes that the order is not original. אֵלֶּה פְקוּדֵי in its present position is preceded by the whole tabernacle *including* the furniture; but Num. iv. 28 and 33 tell us that Ithamar superintended the service of the Gershonites and Merarites who together were responsible for everything *except* the furniture. The furniture was the charge of the Kohathites and Num. iii. 32 expressly says that the Kohathites were under the supervision not of Ithamar but of Eleazar. Originally, Popper claims, the Hebrew text was so arranged that no mention of the furniture preceded the phrase אֵלֶּה פְקוּדֵי; but subsequently the proper significance of אֵלֶּה פְקוּדֵי was lost sight of, the text rearranged, and אֵלֶּה פְקוּדֵי was mistakenly referred to the list of materials which now follows it in the M.T.

Popper next examines the Greek and finds that it fits this interpretation exactly. It gives אֵלֶּה פְקוּדֵי the meaning 'this is the arrangement' and not 'this is the sum', and the text is so ordered that no mention of the furniture precedes its αὕτη ἡ σύνταξις. Instead the things that were under Ithamar's supervision come first with αὕτη ἡ σύνταξις as a concluding note; then follows ch. xxxviii with its account of the furniture which was under Eleazar's care. Popper concludes, therefore, that the Greek order is correct and based on the original Hebrew text, the order of which has been unintelligently perverted in the M.T.

This explanation is attractive for its simplicity and ingenuity, but upon further investigation it breaks down. To start with, it is based on a misconstruing of the Hebrew. The phrase 'the service of the Levites by the hand of Ithamar' is placed in the Hebrew in simple apposition to the previous part of the sentence, 'this is the reckoning...which was made by the command of Moses'. McNeile rightly says, p. 235, 'their service consisted, in this instance, of drawing up the reckoning'. The verse is well translated by Addis (*Documents of the Hexateuch*, vol. II, p. 285) 'This is the reckoning of (the things for) the tabernacle, the tabernacle of the testimony, which reckoning was made by the command of Moses, by the help of the Levites under the superintendence of Ithamar, the son of Aaron, the priest'. And with this Moffatt's freer rendering agrees: 'Here follows a note of the various amounts needed for the Dwelling... drawn up, at the bidding of Moses, by the Levites under the supervision of Ithamar....' The Revised Version, on the other hand, is wrong: 'This is the sum of the things for the tabernacle ...as they were counted according to the commandment of Moses, *for* the service of the Levites....' The addition of *for* is gratuitous; the Hebrew has no preposition. Now the Greek also has a similar mistake: ...τὴν λειτουργίαν εἶναι τῶν Λευιτῶν...; and this raises the possibility that while the Hebrew did not intend this 'service' to refer to the arrangements detailed in Num. iii and iv, the Greek may have misunderstood its Hebrew in this sense. The test will be whether the Greek has in fact arranged its material to agree with the plan of Num. iii and iv. If it has, αὕτη ἡ σύνταξις will refer to ch. xxxvii, which should then give us the items that were under Ithamar's superintendence. Actually, ch. xxxvii is far from giving us all the items that Ithamar supervised: it omits the goats'-hair curtains, skin coverings, frames and bases, all of which were major parts of his charge. On the other hand ch. xxxviii which comes *after* αὕτη ἡ σύνταξις mentions the frames, bars, pillars, hooks, 'capitals' (bases) and pins, all of which likewise came according to Numbers under Ithamar's supervision. And yet again, ch. xxxviii mentions these things in the middle of its account of the furniture which came not under Ithamar's but under Eleazar's control. So on Popper's own theory the Greek order is as mistaken and inaccurate as the Hebrew and cannot be original.

We conclude therefore that neither the Hebrew nor the Greek intended its order to reproduce the organisation of Num. iii and iv; that the term אֵלֶּה פְקוּדֵי does not mean what Popper says it means, but what it has always been taken to mean, namely, 'this is the sum', and that it refers to the summary of workmen and materials that follows it; that the Hebrew order as it now stands in ch. xxxviii. 21–31 of the M.T. is original; and that the Greek's division of the corresponding paragraph into two parts (xxxvii. 19–21, xxxix. 1–9) by the insertion of ch. xxxviii was not authorized by its Hebrew *Vorlage*, and was not the work of the original translator, but of the later editor of ch. xxxviii.

2. THE POSITION OF THE VESTMENTS

But a still more remarkable thing must be noticed. The paragraph which ch. xxxviii in the Greek interrupts gives a summary of the metals used in the making of the tabernacle—gold, silver, copper (in that order). When it is finished the M.T. proceeds immediately to describe the making of the vestments. It is here that the biggest difference in order between the Hebrew and the Greek occurs, and we shall need to examine the context in both closely.

Greek	M.T.
xxxix. 1–9	xxxviii. 24–31
List of metals	List of metals
xxxix. 10	
καὶ τὸ παράθεμα τὸ χαλκοῦν τοῦ θυσιαστηρίου καὶ πάντα	

τὰ σκεύη τοῦ θυσιαστηρίου καὶ
πάντα τὰ ἐργαλεῖα τῆς σκηνῆς
τοῦ μαρτυρίου.

xxxix. 11
καὶ ἐποίησαν οἱ υἱοὶ Ισραηλ
καθὰ συνέταξεν Κύριος τῷ
Μωυσῇ, οὕτως ἐποίησαν.

xxxix. 12
τὸ δὲ λοιπὸν χρυσίον τοῦ
ἀφαιρέματος ἐποίησαν σκεύη
εἰς τὸ λειτουργεῖν ἐν αὐτοῖς
ἔναντι Κυρίου.

xxxix. 13
καὶ τὴν καταλειφθεῖσαν ὑάκινθον καὶ πορφύραν καὶ τὸ κόκκινον ἐποίησαν στολὰς λειτουργικὰς Ααρων ὥστε λειτουρ-
γεῖν ἐν αὐταῖς ἐν τῷ ἁγίῳ.

xxxix. 1
And of the blue, and purple
and scarlet, they made finely
wrought garments[1] for ministering in the holy place, *and
made the holy garments for Aaron;
as the Lord commanded Moses.*

xxxix. 14
καὶ ἤνεγκαν τὰς στολὰς πρὸς
Μωυσῆν καὶ τὴν σκηνήν. . . .

Certain things are at once obvious: the Greek list xxxix. 1–9
follows closely the M.T. list xxxviii. 24–31. The M.T. follows
on immediately with the vestments; the Greek has three extra
verses, the origin of which we must leave for the moment,
while we observe that, beyond shadow of doubt, the Greek
xxxix. 13 represents the first part (the part that is not italicized)
of the M.T. xxxix. 1. Thereafter the Greek continues not with
the vestments, but with a list of finished articles, which in the
M.T. comes *after* the account of the vestments (Heb. xxxix. 33).
So it appears that the Greek parts company with the M.T. in
what is, for the M.T., the middle of a verse. That in itself is
strange.

The account of the vestments in the Greek is given in ch. xxxvi,
and when we compare the Hebrew and Greek contexts to dis-

---

[1] Not as A.V., cloths *of service*. The A.V. has made the same mistake as the
Greek, taking שרד for שרת.

cover the exact point of departure, we find the following state of affairs:

Greek	M.T.
xxxvi. 1–7	equals xxxvi. 1–7
xxxvi. 8	xxxvi. 8
καὶ ἐποίησεν πᾶς σοφὸς ἐν τοῖς ἐργαζομένοις τὰς στολὰς τῶν ἁγίων αἵ εἰσιν Ααρων τῷ ἱερεῖ, καθὰ συνέταξεν Κύριος τῷ Μωυσῇ.	And every wise-hearted man among them that wrought the work made the tabernacle with ten curtains, of fine twined linen....

Once more the Greek parts company with the M.T. in the middle of a verse. The verse comes at the end of a section in which the Greek has been following the M.T. very closely. Both begin exactly the same: but while the M.T. proceeds to tell of the tabernacle curtains, the Greek introduces the vestments. The remarkable thing is that the second part of the Greek verse, from τὰς στολάς onwards, is a translation of the second part of the M.T. verse, xxxix. 1 (the part italicized above), which introduces the making of the vestments. In other words the Greek xxxvi. 8 = the M.T. xxxvi. 8a + xxxix. 1b. This means that if we took the Greek xxxvi. 8 from τὰς στολάς onwards and all that follows it down to the end of ch. xxxvi, and put it immediately after the Greek xxxix. 13 (supplying only καὶ ἐποίησαν as copula), we should have in Greek a sentence that exactly corresponded to the M.T. xxxix. 1:

Greek	M.T.
xxxix. 13	xxxix. 1
καὶ τὴν καταλειφθεῖσαν ὑάκινθον καὶ πορφύραν καὶ τὸ κόκκινον ἐποίησαν στολὰς λειτουργικὰς [Ααρων] ὥστε λειτουργεῖν ἐν αὐταῖς ἐν τῷ ἁγίῳ.	And of the blue and purple and scarlet they made finely wrought garments for ministering in the holy place, and made the holy garments for Aaron, as the Lord commanded Moses.
xxxvi. 8b	
⟨καὶ ἐποίησαν⟩ τὰς στολὰς τῶν ἁγίων, αἵ εἰσιν Ααρων [τῷ ἱερεῖ], καθὰ συνέταξεν Κύριος τῷ Μωυσῇ.	
xxxvi. 9–40[1]	equals xxxix. 2–31

[1] B.M.'s numeration.

and, at the same time, the account of the making of the vestments would come in the Greek exactly where it now comes in the M.T.

Now the fact that the Greek can be rearranged so easily and neatly, and, when rearranged, agrees so exactly with the M.T., shows at once that this big difference in order between the Hebrew and the Greek does not go back to a Hebrew text vastly different from the M.T. On the contrary it is evident that the text followed by the Greek must have been exceedingly close to the M.T.; only, either that Hebrew text stood in the same order as the Greek does now, or else the Greek once stood in the order that the M.T. has now, with its two phrases xxxix. 13 and xxxvi. 8b standing together as a single verse. Surprisingly, there is evidence enough to settle this question; it is the Greek order that has changed.

First of all we may observe that the Greek phrase xxxix. 13 does not now make sense, whereas it makes excellent sense the moment it is followed by xxxvi. 8b and the making of the vestments. It says καὶ τὴν καταλειφθεῖσαν ὑάκινθον... though there is nothing in the Hebrew corresponding to καταλειφθεῖσαν. καταλειφθεῖσαν, however, is original and was introduced when the Greek followed the Hebrew order; it made sense then, but does not now that the Greek order has been changed. An analogy will help us to see the point. In Exod. xxix. 10 ff. we get the details of the slaying of the bullock at the priests' induction. Verse 12 says, 'And thou shalt take of the bullock's blood and put it on the horns of the altar with thy finger'. Then the Hebrew continues, 'and all the blood thou shalt pour out at the base of the altar'. The translator felt a difficulty—how could *all* the blood be poured out at the base of the altar, if some had already been put on the horns? So he wrote τὸ δὲ λοιπὸν πᾶν αἷμα ἐκχεεῖς (and all *the rest of* the blood thou shalt pour out). λοιπόν has nothing to correspond with it in the Hebrew: it is an explanatory addition. Similarly with καταλειφθεῖσαν in xxxix. 13. The Hebrew (xxxix. 1) merely says, 'And of the blue and purple and scarlet they made'...the vestments. But the translator again felt a difficulty: earlier chapters had described the use of some of the blue, purple and scarlet to make the tabernacle curtains, two veils and court-gate. So once more he made an explanatory addition: the vestments, according to him, were made out of the *remaining* blue, purple and scarlet.[1] Since subsequently the making of the vestments has been transferred in the Greek to ch. xxxvi, everything made of blue, purple and scarlet has already been mentioned before the Greek comes to ch. xxxix. 16; and moreover, the use of the materials for the vestments now comes *before* their use for the curtains and veils. To say, therefore, as ch. xxxix. 14 now does, that of the *remaining* blue, purple and scarlet they made the robes for use in the service of the holy place, is utterly pointless—remaining from what? It could only make sense if the στολαί of ch. xxxix. 13 were thought of as additional to those mentioned in ch. xxxvi; but this is manifestly not the meaning either of the Greek or of the Hebrew which the Greek xxxix. 13 is meant to translate.

Popper, indeed, maintains, pp. 160–3, that these στολαί *were* additional to the priests' vestments, and were in fact the cloths used to cover the sacred vessels on the march (see Num. iv); and he quotes Josephus in support of his interpretation. But whatever Josephus in later times thought, the original LXX did not so understand the Hebrew. The choice of term—στολαί—and the unnecessarily emphatic translation—ὥστε λειτουργεῖν ἐν αὐταῖς ἐν τῷ ἁγίῳ—show that the translator understood the στολαί to be robes with which the priests were clothed when they ministered in the holy place, and not cloths to cover the vessels on the march through the desert. Popper also points out that, in the list in xxxix. 14ff., the Greek mentions the στολαί (which he claims are coverings) in *v.* 14 and the priests' vestments later in *v.* 19. He claims that this separation proves that the στολαί of *v.* 14 are different things from the στολαί of *v.* 19. But comparison with the Hebrew (xxxix. 33) will show that the Greek is, as we have observed before (p. 73), either mistaken or corrupt. The Hebrew is giving a list of the components of the tabernacle as they were brought on completion to Moses. Its order is natural and its use of technical terms precise. 'They brought the tabernacle (=the ten linen curtains)...the tent (=the eleven goats'-hair curtains) and all the instruments thereof, the clasps thereof (which fastened the curtains together),

---

[1] These explanatory insertions, occurring one of them in the first section and the other in the second section, betray the same meticulous mind. They are further evidence that the first and second sections are by the same translator.

the frames thereof (over which the curtains were spread), the bars thereof (which kept the frames together)....' The Greek order is τὰς στολὰς...τὴν σκηνὴν καὶ τὰ σκεύη αὐτῆς.... Whatever the στολάς are here, they are evidently out of place. But if they are, as Popper maintains, the cloths that covered the sacred vessels on the march, to mention them first in the list along with the big structural components of the building is absurdly inappropriate. στολάς therefore is certainly wrong; it is probably corrupt. In consequence Popper loses his supporting argument, and we return to the conclusion that στολάς in xxxix. 13 is meant to refer to the vestments, and that κατα- λειφθεῖσαν is a now meaningless relic of the days when the Greek followed the order of the Hebrew.

This conclusion is confirmed by yet another consideration. In xxxv. 19 the M.T. uses three phrases in speaking of the vestments:

(1) finely wrought garments for ministering in the holy place,
(2) the holy garments for Aaron the priest,
(3) the garments of his sons, to minister in the priests' office.

The Greek, xxxv. 18, 19, has all three phrases though it changes their order:

(2) τὰς στολὰς τὰς ἁγίας Ααρων τοῦ ἱερέως,
(1) τὰς στολὰς ἐν αἷς λειτουργήσουσιν ἐν αὐταῖς (+ἐν τῷ ἁγίῳ AFM+majority),
(3) τοὺς χιτῶνας τοῖς υἱοῖς Ααρων τῆς ἱερατείας.

In xxxix. 1 the M.T. mentions only two items:

(1) finely wrought garments for ministering in the holy place,
(2) holy garments for Aaron.

The third item is appropriately mentioned later on in *v.* 27:

(3) coats of fine linen of woven work for Aaron and for his sons.

When we piece together the now scattered fragments in the Greek we find that xxxix. 13 is really the first phrase, xxxvi. 8b the second and xxxvi. 35 the third, thus:

(1) xxxix. 13 στολὰς λειτουργικὰς Ααρων ὥστε λειτουργεῖν ἐν αὐταῖς ἐν τῷ ἁγίῳ,
(2) xxxvi. 8b στολὰς τῶν ἁγίων, αἵ εἰσιν Ααρων τῷ ἱερεῖ,

(3) xxxvi. 35 χιτῶνας βυσσίνους ἔργον ὑφαντὸν Ααρων καὶ τοῖς υἱοῖς αὐτοῦ.

This shows clearly that the Greek xxxix. 13 + xxxvi. 8b together represent exactly the M.T. xxxix. 1 and that the στολαί of xxxix. 13 (Gk.) are not completely different things from the garments described in ch. xxxvi (Heb. xxxix) as Popper would have us believe.

Moreover there is further evidence that it is the Greek and not the Hebrew order that has suffered change. The excision of the account of the priests' vestments from its original context, and its removal elsewhere, left some floating debris in the Greek text which subsequently drifted into places where it did not properly belong. In the M.T. the order is: the summary of materials followed by the making of the vestments (xxxviii. 21–xxxix. 31). The account of the vestments finishes with the phrase, v. 31, 'as the Lord commanded Moses'. Verse 32 follows immediately and appropriately, 'Thus was finished all the work of the tabernacle of the tent of meeting: and the children of Israel did according to all that the Lord commanded Moses, so did they'. Verse 33 follows, again very naturally, 'And they brought the tabernacle unto Moses...'. Now we turn to the Greek, to find the Greek equivalents. For two of the verses, vv. 31 and 33, the Greek equivalents are easily found, in xxxvi. 40 and xxxix. 14 respectively:

Greek	M.T.
xxxvi. 40	xxxix. 31
καὶ ἐπέθηκαν ἐπ᾽ αὐτὸ λῶμα ὑακίνθινον, ὥστε ἐπικεῖσθαι ἐπὶ τὴν μίτραν ἄνωθεν ὃν τρόπον συνέταξεν Κύριος τῷ Μωυσῇ.	And they tied unto it a lace of blue to fasten it upon the mitre above; as the Lord commanded Moses.
xxxix. 14	xxxix. 33
καὶ ἤνεγκαν τὰς στολὰς πρὸς Μωυσῆν καὶ τὴν σκηνὴν καὶ τὰ σκεύη αὐτῆς καὶ τὰς βάσεις καὶ τοὺς μοχλοὺς αὐτῆς καὶ τοὺς στύλους.	And they brought the tabernacle unto Moses, the tent, and all its furniture, its clasps, its frames, its bars and its pillars and its bases.

That leaves the equivalent of xxxix. 32 to be found. The second half of this verse is undoubtedly represented by the Greek xxxix. 11.

Greek	M.T.
xxxix. 11	xxxix. 32
καὶ ἐποίησαν οἱ υἱοὶ Ισραηλ καθὰ συνέταξεν Κύριος τῷ Μωυσῆ, οὕτως ἐποίησαν.	Thus was finished all the work of the tabernacle of the tent of meeting: *and the children of Israel did according to all that the Lord commanded Moses, so did they.*

Naturally we should expect the first part of the Hebrew verse to be represented by the Greek xxxix. 10, if it is represented at all. But xxxix. 10 in the Greek appears to be the last verse of the list of articles that were made from the copper-offering. It runs: καὶ τὸ παράθεμα τὸ χαλκοῦν τοῦ θυσιαστηρίου καὶ πάντα τὰ σκεύη τοῦ θυσιαστηρίου, καὶ πάντα τὰ ἐργαλεῖα τῆς σκηνῆς τοῦ μαρτυρίου. Now the M.T. likewise has this list of articles, and, when it is compared with the Greek, the two lists agree except in the following points:

(1) The Greek omits the copper altar, although it has the grate. The reason is that the list has been edited to make it agree with the Greek account in ch. xxxviii, which says the altar was made, not from the copper-offering but from the rebels' censers.

(2) The position of the grate and altar utensils in the Greek list is different. They come at the end (*v.* 10).[1]

(3) The last phrase of all in the Greek, καὶ πάντα τὰ ἐργαλεῖα τῆς σκηνῆς τοῦ μαρτυρίου, has nothing to represent it in the M.T. list at all. When the phrase is examined more closely, its origin becomes apparent. ἐργαλεῖα is the normal translation of עֲבֹדָה; and we have only to supply καὶ συνετελέσθη at the beginning of the phrase to have a translation of the first half of the M.T. xxxix. 32.

Greek	M.T.
xxxix. 10b	xxxix. 32
⟨καὶ συνετελέσθη⟩ πάντα τὰ ἐργαλεῖα τῆς σκηνῆς τοῦ μαρτυρίου.	Thus was finished all the work of the tabernacle of the tent of meeting; and the children of
xxxix. 11	Israel did according to all that
καὶ ἐποίησαν οἱ υἱοὶ Ισραηλ καθὰ συνέταξεν Κύριος τῷ Μωυσῆ, οὕτως ἐποίησαν.	the Lord commanded Moses, so did they.

[1] It is tempting to surmise that the Greek order is accounted for by a desire to group like things with like: the three sets of βάσεις, the two sets of πασσάλους and then the πάντα τὰ σκεύη τοῦ θυσιαστηρίου with the πάντα

The deductions to be made from this are obvious: the con-fusion of xxxix. 10b with xxxix. 10a in the Greek was caused by the excision of the account of the vestments. The matter can best be illustrated in tabular form:

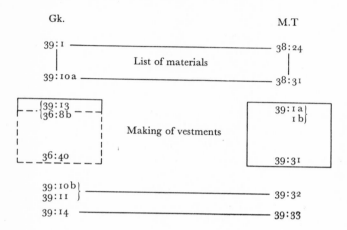

The account of the vestments in the Greek was removed in a block (what is now xxxvi. 8b–xxxvi. 40). That left the intro-ductory sentence of the vestments to become what is now xxxix. 13, and allowed xxxix. 10b to become fused with xxxix. 10a, where it now appears to fit quite well, although originally it had nothing to do with it at all.

There remains the Greek xxxix. 12 to be accounted for. It has no support in the M.T. anywhere; but judged by no other standard than the order of the Greek text itself, this verse is out of place. After describing the uses to which the metals were put the Greek list (xxxix. 1–10) is rounded off by xxxix. 11 'And the children of Israel did as the Lord commanded Moses, so did they'. Then *v.* 12 appears to make a fresh start with some more metal: 'And of the rest of the gold of the offering they made....' It is manifestly out of place.

The Greek text has thus suffered a serious dislocation since it was first composed. Originally the making of the vestments

τὰ ἐργαλεῖα τῆς σκηνῆς because, to an unsuspecting editor, they would appear to be similar. Actually, as we are about to see, the ἐργαλεῖα τῆς σκηνῆς had originally nothing to do with this list at all.

stood in the Greek in ch. xxxix. 13 ff., that is, in the same place as it still occupies in the M.T. The present order does not mean that the original translator used a text that in this respect differed from the M.T.; it is the result of editorial rearrangement, a rearrangement that was inefficiently and clumsily done, but which on that account betrays itself the more clearly.

We have demonstrated, then, that in the Greek both the position of the furniture (ch. xxxviii) and that of the vestments are the result of editing. We have moreover shown that vestments once stood in the same position in the Greek as they do in the M.T. It is but a small step further to suppose that the account of the furniture (or at least so much of it as the original translator gave) likewise once stood in the same position in the Greek as in the M.T. Some confirmation of this step is afforded by the list in xxxix. 14–21 (xxxix. 33–41). As we have seen (pp. 81 f.), this list groups together at the end many of the soft fabrics in the manner of chs. xxxvi and xxxvii. Doubtless this arrangement of the list is deliberate, but we need if possible to discover whether this arrangement is original or not, and if not what was its original arrangement. We shall find that the present order is not original but that the list once followed the same order as the M.T. It is likely, therefore, that the furniture and textiles in chs. xxxvii and xxxviii stood, before their rearrangement, in the same order as the M.T.

From all we know of the original translator's methods, it is most unlikely that he translated his Hebrew (whatever it was) in full; so that the omission of such things as the mercy-seat may well be due to his abbreviation. But one of the three phrases relating to the vestments is also missing, and that is surprising in view of the prominence given to the vestments in this list by their position at the head of the textile group. The M.T. as usual has all three phrases (xxxix. 41):

(1) finely wrought garments for ministering in the holy place,
(2) the holy garments for Aaron the priest,
(3) the garments of his sons to minister in the priests' office.

The Greek of xxxix. 19 has nos. 2 and 3 exactly:

(2) τὰς στολὰς τοῦ ἁγίου αἵ εἰσιν Ααρων,
(3) τὰς στολὰς τῶν υἱῶν αὐτοῦ εἰς τὴν ἱερατείαν,

but it lacks (1) completely. Interestingly enough *v.* 13 is this phrase no. 1, but we have already seen that it originally stood at the head of the account of the making of the vestments. And anyway the list here does not begin till *v.* 14. Again, the list begins with the mention of στολαί of some kind; but this reference as we have seen (pp. 89f.) is either a mistranslation or a corruption. So the Greek list is short of one phrase relating to the vestments, which it is unlikely to have been, if the original translator had been responsible for giving the vestments prominence.

Then there is a curious and unnecessary repetition. After the screen for the gate of the court the M.T. has: 'the cords thereof and the pins thereof, and all the instruments of the service of the tabernacle for the tent of meeting'. The Greek has first: καὶ πάντα τὰ σκεύη τῆς σκηνῆς καὶ πάντα τὰ ἐργαλεῖα αὐτῆς, which could conceivably be an abbreviated paraphrase of the Hebrew, and then later in the verse: καὶ τοὺς πασσάλους καὶ πάντα τὰ ἐργαλεῖα τὰ εἰς τὰ ἔργα τῆς σκηνῆς τοῦ μαρτυρίου, which is a full translation of the Hebrew except for the omission of τοὺς κάλους αὐτῆς at the beginning and of τῆς σκέπης after σκηνῆς. There is evidently some unnecessary duplication here, possibly resulting from the conflation of an earlier and later translation; certainly both phrases would not have stood in the original translation. But the most interesting feature is that it is between these two phrases that the Greek has now the skin coverings. Their position is at once suspect. They are placed here apparently to be in company with the soft fabrics—the vestments, door-screen, gate-screen, and court-hangings, whereas the M.T. has them along with the tabernacle and tent which they served to cover. The actual Greek words are: καὶ τὰς διφθέρας δέρματα κριῶν ἠρυθροδανωμένα καὶ τὰ καλύμματα δέρματα ὑακίνθινα καὶ τῶν λοιπῶν τὰ ἐπικαλύμματα. They include the covering of rams' skins and the covering of sealskins, both of which we recognize immediately from the Hebrew. But what are 'the coverings of the remaining things', τῶν λοιπῶν τὰ ἐπικαλύμματα? As they stand, one would think that they were coverings in similar sense as the rams' skins and seal-skins with which they are grouped, and that this fact accounted for the grouping. Actually they are nothing of the kind, for, as many scholars have seen, the Greek xxxix. 21 is in part a

95

translation of the Hebrew xxix. 34 and the phrase τῶν λοιπῶν τὰ ἐπικαλύμματα refers to the veil. It will help to put the Greek and Hebrew together:

וְאֶת־מִכְסֵה עוֹרֹת הָאֵילִם הַמְאָדָּמִים
καὶ τὰς διφθέρας δέρματα κριῶν ἠρυθροδανωμένα

וְאֶת־מִכְסֵה עֹרֹת הַתְּחָשִׁים
καὶ τὰ καλύμματα δέρματα ὑακίνθινα

וְאֵת פָּרֹכֶת הַמָּסָךְ׃
καὶ τῶν λοιπῶν τὰ ἐπικαλύμματα.

We notice that the Greek throughout follows the Hebrew very closely, putting a word-for-word equivalent in exactly the same order. Quite in the manner of the original translator, however, מִכְסֵה is given two different renderings. Moreover the singular מִכְסֵה is rendered on both occasions by a plural which prepares us for a plural, τὰ ἐπικαλύμματα, as the equivalent for הַמָּסָךְ. The meticulous order of the Greek throughout and particularly in the third phrase puts it beyond doubt that λοιπῶν stands for פָּרֹכֶת. As a translation it is outrageous, and it is possible that the translator misread his Hebrew, or else that his original rendering has become corrupt. Elsewhere, xxxv. 11 (12) and xl. 19 (21), he renders אֶת פָּרֹכֶת הַמָּסָךְ once simply τὸ κατα-πέτασμα and once fully τὸ κατακάλυμμα τοῦ καταπετάσματος. Nevertheless, after his varying translations of 'capital', 'fillet', 'base' and 'hook' (see pp. 21f., 44f.) it is not at all unlikely that he deliberately put λοιπῶν for פָּרֹכֶת here. But however it is, whether λοιπῶν is original or corrupt, it is certain that τῶν λοιπῶν τὰ ἐπικαλύμματα represents the Hebrew for 'the veil of the screen', that is, the curtain that screened the holy of holies from the holy place.

That being so, we can decide with a fair amount of confidence what was the original position of the skins and veil in the Greek list. That the veil comes immediately after the skins in the M.T. order is reasonable enough, since the M.T. first gives the structure—tabernacle, tent, clasps, frames, coverings and veil—and then deals with the furniture, starting from the inside and working out. Moreover the veil hung 'under the clasps' (Heb. xxvi. 33) which held the tabernacle curtains together. It is reasonable, then, that the M.T. should have the veil grouped with the tabernacle, tent and skins. It is noticeable however that the M.T. does *not* put together the screen for the door and the screen for the gate. They come, consistently with the M.T.'s obvious plan, in *vv.* 38 and 40 respectively. The Greek, however, puts these two screens together,[1] *v.* 20, τὸ καταπέτασμα τῆς θύρας τῆς σκηνῆς καὶ τῆς πύλης τῆς αὐλῆς, and that closely with the vestments and court hangings: the Greek is grouping like things. Then, sandwiched between that curious repetition we have just discussed (p. 95), come the skin coverings and τῶν λοιπῶν τὰ ἐπικαλύμματα; so that the Greek has in fact grouped the fabrics in this order: vestments, court hangings, screens of door and gate, skin coverings and veil-screen. This shows surely that whoever is responsible for this order could not have realized that τῶν λοιπῶν τὰ ἐπικαλύμματα really represented the veil. The veil was a καταπέτασμα as was the screen (καταπέτασμα, *v.* 20) for the door and that for the gate; indeed, it was the καταπέτασμα *par excellence*. No one would knowingly have grouped this veil last in a list which puts together the other καταπετάσματα, and arranges the fabrics in a roughly descending order of interest and importance. On the other hand it is easy to see how an editor, interested in grouping the fabrics together, found the skin coverings and τῶν λοιπῶν τὰ ἐπικαλύμματα standing at the beginning where the M.T. still has them, and moved them just as they were to the end of his fabrics group, not realizing what τῶν λοιπῶν τὰ ἐπικαλύμματα really were. Taking them at their face value as coverings, perhaps for the vessels, he would quite happily put them at the end of his list. This also would account for the fact that the skins and veil are grouped with the fabrics, but the tabernacle curtains and the tent curtains not. It would not readily occur to an editor, who saw (whatever stood originally for) στολάς and σκηνήν at the head of the list, that the tabernacle and tent were between them the twenty-one most important curtains in the whole structure.

We conclude, then, that this list once stood in roughly the same order as the M.T. and was rearranged by an editor who did not fully realize the significance of the Hebrew that lay behind the original translation. That in itself is interesting, for

[1] Cf. the putting together of the staves for ark and table in xxxviii. 11 of the Greek.

we have noticed the same feature about the list in ch. xxxviii. 18–20. It, too, was compiled by someone who did not understand the proper meaning of the Hebrew behind the original translation (p. 50).[1] But we must leave discussion of this editor to the next chapter. Our main result here is that the similarity between the present position of the fabrics and furniture in chs. xxxvii and xxxviii and the present position of the fabrics in the list in xxxix. 14–21 suggests a common hand behind both; and inasmuch as the list once agreed with the M.T. order, it is most probable that the fabrics and furniture once stood in the M.T. order, just as we have demonstrated that the vestments did. And this means that in all major respects the original translation of the second section followed the same order as the M.T.[2]

[1] Cf. also the suggestion, p. 92 n., that the present order of the Greek list xxxix. 8–10 is the work of someone who did not realize what the Hebrew was underlying πάντα τὰ ἐργαλεῖα τῆς σκηνῆς.

[2] In Appendix I the Greek text of chs. xxxv–xl is set out in its suggested original order.

CHAPTER XI

THE SUMMING-UP

It remains just to draw together our conclusions and to consider their implications.

1. TRANSLATION

(1) Differences in the translation of technical terms were found insufficient to prove that the second section (apart from ch. xxxviii) was by a different translator from the first section. Rather such differences proved to be the normal style, not only of Exodus, but of all the technical portions of the Pentateuch (Chs. ii and v).

(2) At the same time there were striking similarities of translation that made it evident that both sections were by the same translator (pp. 37 f., 89 n.).

(3) Chapter xxxviii, however, in its present form proved to be the work of a later editor (Chs. v and vi).

2. CONTENT

(4) Differences in content were considerable, but the liberties taken with the text by the second section were different in size only and not in principle from those taken by the first section (p. 76).

(5) It was found that omissions in the Greek could not be taken to imply corresponding omissions in the Hebrew text followed by the translator. On the contrary, the omissions, mistranslations and additions not seldom reduced the Greek account to an absurdity of which no original Hebrew composition[1] could possibly have been guilty (pp. 45, 48–50, 73).

(6) Moreover the omission of the account of the making of the golden altar, about which much has been said in the past,

---

[1] I.e. as distinct from Hebrew texts that may have 'run wild'. It is possible, of course, that the Greek has in places followed a 'wild' Hebrew text; but it seems unnecessary to suppose this, when so many of the Greek's peculiarities can definitely be traced to the Greek translator and editor.

proved to be without the significance hitherto assigned to it (pp. 66f.).

(7) Then it was observed that the Greek of the second section, in spite of its abbreviations, paraphrases and major differences of order, was following in its detailed order a Hebrew text materially the same as the M.T.; and, that being so, the most reasonable way to explain the proportions of the translation of the second section was to assume that it was in the main by the same translator as the first section (pp. 75–6).

3. ORDER

(8) The major differences in order between the Greek and the M.T. we discovered were caused by a rearrangement of the original Greek text. They did not imply another Hebrew text arranged in the same order as the Greek now follows (Ch. x).

4. GENERAL DEDUCTIONS

(9) From all this it becomes clear that we are not warranted to suppose that chs. xxxv–xl were missing in the Hebrew text used by the original translator.

(10) There is likewise no evidence to suggest that the translator regarded chs. xxxv–xl as less sacrosanct than the rest of the book, or that the translation was made from a Hebrew text that had not reached its present form and order.

(11) And if the present Greek order evidences, as some claim, a special interest in the priesthood, that interest cannot be charged upon the original LXX, still less upon its pre-Masoretic *Vorlage*.

5. THE LATER EDITOR

It will be helpful, finally, to piece together what evidence we have about the date, motives and methods of the editor who is responsible for the present order of the text.

About the date it can be certainly said that the editing was done before Origen, for the text which Origen corrects is the 'altered' text. Moreover, to stand as it does in all our MSS., the alteration must have been made very early indeed and very near the fountain from which the stream of the Greek text has flowed.

The editor's motives can hardly be judged separately from his methods. Doubtless the desire to improve and complete the original translation played some part, but by itself it would not account for the change of order. Swete's suggestion (Introd. p. 235) that the change in order[1] was designed to give precedence to the ornaments of the priesthood would account for the position of the vestments in ch. xxxvi; but it would not account for the position of the court hangings, gate and pillars in ch. xxxvii before the furniture in ch. xxxviii, nor for the position of the vestments in the list in xxxv. 10–19. Finn's suggestion (p. 469) that the Greek grouping is according to the materials comes nearer to satisfying the evidence: everything requiring the use of soft fabrics has been described before the furniture is mentioned in ch. xxxviii; the placing of ch. xxxviii in its present position makes this fabrics section conclude with a reference to Eliab, the chief worker in fabrics; the list in xxxix. 14 ff. groups the fabrics together; the 'special passage' in ch. xxxviii. 18–20 is a list of metalwork; and after the furniture group in ch. xxxviii the Greek puts together the four 'lists' (pp. 80–2). Against this theory it may be argued that the fabrics group contains references (in ch. xxxvii) to other things, such as the pillars and bases, and the objection is valid so far as it goes. The truth about the whole matter is that while order of a kind can be perceived behind the rearrangement of the Greek text, the order is very general and the rearrangement is only roughly done. And what is true of the main order is true of the detailed work. Chapter xxxviii. 18–20 is very unsatisfactory and incomplete, judged only as a list of metalwork which it clearly intends to be (pp. 47–51), let alone its howlers. Then no attempt has been made to reconcile its detailed information with the surrounding chapters, or to avoid needless repetition (pp. 40–1). Again the rearrangement of the list in xxxix. 14 f. to group together the fabrics is imperfectly done and, seen in the light of the Hebrew which the list originally translated, it borders on the absurd. And both this list and the one in xxxviii. 18–20 show that the editor either did not know Hebrew well, or else did not trouble to consult the Hebrew underlying the original before rearranging the Greek. We therefore may not expect the present Greek order to reveal some consistent, highly detailed and accurately worked out plan; such a feat was beyond the intention, if not the ability, of the editor.

[1] Which he of course attributes to the original translator or to his Hebrew *Vorlage*.

SUGGESTED RESTORATION OF THE GREEK TEXT

The following is an attempted restoration of the original Greek order. It deals with the major points only and not with the smaller details. The numbers used are those of the present order as given in Brooke–McLean. The one omission required by the restored order is marked by square brackets, the two additions by angle brackets.

⎧xxxvi. 8a   καὶ ἐποίησεν πᾶς σοφὸς ἐν τοῖς ἐργαζομένοις [καὶ εποιησαν]
⎩xxxvii. 1   τῇ σκηνῇ δέκα αὐλαίας...

xxxvii. 6   ...καὶ τοὺς στύλους αὐτῶν πέντε καὶ τοὺς κρίκους· καὶ τὰς κεφαλίδας αὐτῶν κατεχρύσωσαν χρυσίῳ καὶ αἱ βάσεις αὐτῶν πέντε χαλκαῖ.

xxxviii. 1   καὶ ἐποίησεν Βεσελεηλ τὴν κιβωτόν...

xxxviii. 26   ...οὗτος ἐποίησεν τὸν λουτῆρα χαλκοῦν καὶ τὴν βάσιν αὐτοῦ χαλκῆν ἐκ τῶν κατόπτρων τῶν νηστευσασῶν αἳ ἐνήστευσαν παρὰ τὰς θύρας τῆς σκηνῆς τοῦ μαρτυρίου ἐν ᾗ ἡμέρᾳ ἔπηξεν αὐτήν.

xxxvii. 7   καὶ ἐποίησαν τὴν αὐλήν· τὰ πρὸς λίβα, ἱστία τῆς αὐλῆς ἐκ βύσσου κεκλωσμένης ἑκατὸν ἐφ᾽ ἑκατόν...

xxxvii. 21   ...καὶ Ελιαβ ὁ τοῦ Αχισαμακ ἐκ τῆς φυλῆς Δαν ὃς ἠρχιτεκτόνησεν τὰ ὑφαντὰ καὶ τὰ ῥαφιδευτὰ καὶ ποικιλτικά, ὑφᾶναι τῷ κοκκίνῳ καὶ τῇ βύσσῳ.

xxxix. 1   πᾶν τὸ χρυσίον ὃ κατειργάσθη εἰς τὰ ἔργα κατὰ πᾶσαν τὴν ἐργασίαν τῶν ἁγίων ἐγένετο χρυσίου τοῦ τῆς ἀπαρχῆς, ἐννέα καὶ εἴκοσι τάλαντα καὶ ἑπτακόσιοι εἴκοσι σίκλοι κατὰ τὸν σίκλον τὸν ἅγιον.

xxxix. 12   τὸ δὲ λοιπὸν χρυσίον τοῦ ἀφαιρέματος ἐποίησαν σκεύη εἰς τὸ λειτουργεῖν ἐν αὐτοῖς ἔναντι Κυρίου.

xxxix. 2   καὶ ἀργυρίου ἀφαίρεμα παρὰ τῶν ἐπεσκεμμένων ἀνδρῶν τῆς συναγωγῆς ἑκατὸν τάλαντα καὶ χίλιοι ἑπτακόσιοι ἑβδομήκοντα πέντε σίκλοι...

xxxix. 8 ...καὶ ἐποίησεν ἐξ αὐτοῦ τὰς βάσεις τῆς θύρας τῆς σκηνῆς τοῦ μαρτυρίου

xxxix. 10a καὶ τὸ παράθεμα τὸ χαλκοῦν τοῦ θυσιαστηρίου καὶ πάντα τὰ σκεύη τοῦ θυσιαστηρίου

xxxix. 9 καὶ τὰς βάσεις τῆς πύλης κύκλῳ, καὶ τὰς βάσεις τῆς πύλης τῆς αὐλῆς, καὶ τοὺς πασσάλους τῆς σκηνῆς, καὶ τοὺς πασσάλους τῆς αὐλῆς κύκλῳ.

⎰ xxxix. 13 καὶ τὴν καταλειφθεῖσαν ὑάκινθον καὶ πορφύραν καὶ τὸ
⎱ xxxvi. 8b κόκκινον ἐποίησαν στολὰς λειτουργικὰς Ααρων, ὥστε λειτουργεῖν ἐν αὐταῖς, ἐν τῷ ἁγίῳ, ⟨καὶ ἐποίησαν⟩ τὰς στολὰς τῶν ἁγίων αἵ εἰσιν Ααρων τῷ ἱερεῖ, καθὰ συνέταξεν Κύριος τῷ Μωυσῇ...

xxxvi. 40 ...καὶ ἐπέθηκαν ἐπ' αὐτὸ λῶμα ὑακίνθινον, ὥστε ἐπικεῖσθαι ἐπὶ τὴν μίτραν ἄνωθεν, ὃν τρόπον συνέταξεν Κύριος τῷ Μωυσῇ.

xxxix. 10b ⟨καὶ συνετελέσθη⟩ πάντα τὰ ἐργαλεῖα τῆς σκηνῆς τοῦ μαρτυρίου.

xxxix. 11 καὶ ἐποίησαν οἱ υἱοὶ Ισραηλ καθὰ συνέταξεν Κύριος τῷ Μωυσῇ, οὕτως ἐποίησαν.

xxxix. 14 καὶ ἤνεγκαν τὰς στολὰς πρὸς Μωυσῆν, καὶ τὴν σκηνὴν καὶ τὰ σκεύη αὐτῆς καὶ τὰς βάσεις καὶ τοὺς μοχλοὺς αὐτῆς καὶ τοὺς στύλους

xxxix. 21b καὶ τὰς διφθέρας δέρματα κριῶν ἠρυθροδανωμένα καὶ τὰ καλύμματα δέρματα ὑακίνθινα καὶ τῶν λοιπῶν τὰ ἐπικαλύμματα

xxxix. 15 καὶ τὴν κιβωτὸν τῆς διαθήκης καὶ τοὺς διωστῆρας αὐτῆς...

xxxix. 18 ...καὶ τὴν τράπεζαν τῆς προθέσεως καὶ πάντα τὰ αὐτῆς σκεύη καὶ τοὺς ἄρτους τοὺς προκειμένους

xxxix. 20 καὶ τὰ ἱστία τῆς αὐλῆς καὶ τοὺς στύλους καὶ τὸ καταπέτασμα τῆς θύρας τῆς σκηνῆς καὶ τῆς πύλης τῆς αὐλῆς

xxxix. 21a καὶ πάντα τὰ σκεύη τῆς σκηνῆς καὶ πάντα τὰ ἐργαλεῖα αὐτῆς

xxxix. 21c καὶ τοὺς πασσάλους καὶ πάντα τὰ ἐργαλεῖα τὰ εἰς τὰ ἔργα τῆς σκηνῆς τοῦ μαρτυρίου

xxxix. 19 καὶ τὰς στολὰς τοῦ ἁγίου αἵ εἰσιν Ααρων, καὶ τὰς στολὰς τῶν υἱῶν αὐτοῦ εἰς τὴν ἱερατείαν.

xxxix. 22 ὃ συνέταξεν Κύριος Μωυσῇ, οὕτως ἐποίησαν οἱ υἱοὶ Ισραηλ πᾶσαν τὴν ἀποσκευήν...

xl. 26 ...καὶ τὸ θυσιαστήριον τῶν καρπωμάτων ἔθηκεν παρὰ τὰς θύρας τῆς σκηνῆς.

xxxviii. 27   καὶ ἐποίησεν[1] τὸν λουτῆρα, ἵνα νίπτωνται ἐξ αὐτοῦ Μωυσῆς καὶ Ααρων καὶ οἱ υἱοὶ αὐτοῦ τὰς χεῖρας αὐτῶν καὶ τοὺς πόδας, εἰσπορευομένων αὐτῶν εἰς τὴν σκηνὴν τοῦ μαρτυρίου· ἢ ὅταν προσπορεύωνται πρὸς τὸ θυσιαστήριον λειτουργεῖν ἐνίπτοντο ἐξ αὐτοῦ, καθάπερ συνέταξεν Κύριος τῷ Μωυσῇ.

xl. 27   καὶ ἔστησεν τὴν αὐλὴν κύκλῳ τῆς σκηνῆς καὶ τοῦ θυσιαστηρίου· καὶ συνετέλεσεν Μωυσῆς πάντα τὰ ἔργα...

xl. 32   ...νεφέλη γὰρ ἦν ἐπὶ τῆς σκηνῆς ἡμέρας, καὶ πῦρ ἦν ἐπ' αὐτῆς νυκτός, ἐναντίον παντὸς Ισραηλ, ἐν πάσαις ταῖς ἀναζυγαῖς αὐτῶν.

[1] Read ἔθηκεν or ἔστησεν instead of ἐποίησεν?

THE MS. EVIDENCE FOR THE
TEXT OF EXODUS

THE problem discussed in the foregoing chapters has for the most part been outside the bounds of the lower criticism; only seldom has it been necessary to choose between variant readings. But the fact is that the lower criticism of the closing chapters of Exodus is itself beset with considerable difficulties. Three major types of text are at once discernible: the Origenic, so different from the rest that Brooke–McLean place it in an appendix at the end of the book; the text of B and its allies, differing more than any from the M.T.; and the text of A and its allies, which is nearer to the M.T. than is the text of B and yet is not under the influence of Origen. It will be of interest here to consider how far the text of the B-group is original and the text of the A-group revised; and how far the A-group text is original and the B-group text is either revised or suffering from careless omissions and mistakes; and what further light, if any, this may shed on the problems already discussed. For the final chapters the difficulties are increased by the original omissions, repetitions and paraphrases which so easily gave rise to early mistakes in the transmission of the text. First then it will be wise to consider briefly the state of the text in the body of the book. The evidence used will be that collected by Brooke–McLean.

I. ORIGENIC WITNESSES

The chief Origenic witnesses are F^bGckm 𝔄 ℭ^c 𝔖. They are easily detected: they follow Origen's revised text of chs. xxxvi. 8–xxxix. 43, which is completely different from the LXX text. F^b, however, differs considerably from the other Origenic MSS.: it often takes its readings from wider sources and not only from the o′ column.

In the earlier chapters a and x are both prominent Origenic witnesses, as is shown by the following examples:

v. 6   φαραω] +εν τη ημερα εκεινη   ckmx 𝔄 𝔖 (sub ⁕ εβρ)

vi. 13 πρός²⁰] pr. προς τους υιους ιηλ και Fᵇᵐᵍ (om. τους)
acmx 𝔄 𝕾 (sub ⁕ σ′ θ′)

ix. 10 ἐναντίον φαραω] pr. και εστησαν ackmx 𝔓 𝕾 (sub ⁕ εβρ)

ix. 21 τά] pr. τους παιδας αυτου και ackmx 𝔄 (pr. ⁕) 𝔓 𝕾 (sub ⁕)

ix. 35 τῷ] εν χειρι ackmx 𝔄 𝔓 𝕾 (pr. α′ σ′)

Later in the book a and x, as we shall presently see, desert the Origenic group and witness to the unrevised text.

In ch. xxviii there is an addition of six verses (corresponding to the M.T. *vv.* 23–8) in the following witnesses: Fᵃˀ ckm 𝔄 ℭᶜ 𝕾 and dpt egjsvz n (G is not extant here). The former group is doubtless directly dependent on Origen again for this addition: the relation of the other MSS. to Origen is not so clear. egj certainly have Origenic readings elsewhere:

v. 8 τοῦτο] +αυτοι cegjx 𝕾 (sub ⁕)

ix. 8 πασάτω] +αυτην acegjkmx 𝔄 𝔅 ℭ (uid) 𝔓 𝕾 (sub ⁕)

ix. 20 τά] pr. τους παιδας αυτου και acegjkm (om. αυτου) x 𝔄 𝔓 𝕾 (sub ⁕ uid)

x. 9 ἡμῶν¹⁰] +πορευσομεθα acegjk 𝔄 𝕾 (sub ⁕)

but they do not follow Origen's text at the end of the book and they have not so many Origenic readings as ckm. The same applies to svz n dpt; probably they gained their Origenic readings indirectly through other revisers; ej are manuscripts with catenae.

2. LUCIANIC WITNESSES

Little that is peculiarly Lucianic is noticeable in the Pentateuch. Lucian's contribution seems concerned largely with small variations and readings culled from the later translators. It is therefore indistinct and difficult to isolate, but in other books of the Pentateuch it is generally thought to be contained to differing extents in the MSS. gn dpt bw.[1]

In Exodus g and n, which elsewhere are so close, stand very much apart from each other. g is found in company with ej

[1] There is strong evidence that Hautsch's classification of the Lucianic manuscripts (*Mitteilungen des Septuaginta*, Unternehmens der Königlichen Gesellschaft der Wissenschaften zu Göttingen, Heft 1) is not the last word. See my Tyndale Lecture for 1954, London, 1955, p. 16.

much more frequently, while n has more agreements with the normal group d p t b w:

viii. 15 ἐβαρύνθη ἡ καρδία] εβαρυνεν την καρδιαν   Fᵃ dnpt
viii. 29 θῦσαι] οπως θυσωσι   dnpt
xvi. 3 ὅταν ἐκαθίσαμεν] οτε εκαθημεθα   dnpt (οτι dp) 𝕬 𝕮 (uid) 𝕾
xvi. 4 συλλέξουσι] συναξουσιν   bdn Phil
xxiii. 2 πλειόνων[1°]] πολλων   bnw Phil Clem Thdt

The readings of b w are much less colourful than in Leviticus and d p t have few variants of importance. n, as usual, is full of readings taken from the later translators, often added to the LXX reading.

iv. 23 λαόν] υ̅υ̅   Fᵇn = M.T. = οι λ͞ο͞
iv. 25 ψῆφον] + πετρινον   n = ?σ'
viii. 29 ἐξαπατῆσαι] παραλογησαι   n = ?α' σ'
ix. 3 θάνατος] λοιμος   n = α' σ'
x. 7 ἢ εἰδέναι βούλει] αρα ουπω οιδας   n 𝕭¹ = α' σ'

While g has the closest connection with e j s v z, sometimes the whole group combines with these MSS. in important variants as for instance

xl. 28 καὶ δόξης κυρίου ἐπλήσθη ἡ σκηνή] η δοξα κ̅υ̅ επλησεν την σκηνην = M.T. bdegjnps (txt) tvz (txt)

Here again the possibility is that several revisers have borrowed from the same source.

3. THE B-GROUP MSS.

To cover the whole book one would have to include in this group the MSS. B a f i r h o q u x; all are found to differing extents and in different combinations in close agreement over important variants. Alexandrinus A, too, is a close member of the group in the earlier chapters (as it is in Leviticus), though it ceases to be after about ch. viii. The sub-groups within this larger group are themselves a heterogeneous collection, but the group as a whole is marked by its very strong witness to a text unadapted to the M.T. as the following readings show:

The group is free from additions according to M.T.

iv. 25 πόδας   BA a fir qu] + αυτου   FM rell 𝕬 𝕭 𝕮 (uid) 𝕷ʳ 𝕾 Cyr

v. 10 ἐργοδιῶκται   BA a fir o bw]+του λαου   FM rell 𝔄𝔅ℭ𝔖
vii. 5 χεῖρα   BA* hoqu]+μου   A¹FM rell 𝔄𝔅𝔏ʳ𝔖
viii. 31 τῶν   B ir o qu s] pr. απο   AM rell 𝔅𝔖
xxxi. 10 ἱερατεύειν   B a i*rh kx] pr. εις το   AFᵇMiᵃ rell
xxxii. 11 θεοῦ   B a fir oqu x] om. h:+αυτου   AM rell 𝔄𝔅ℭ𝔏ʳ𝔖 Cyr ed
xxxv. 3 τῇ ἡμέρᾳ   B a fi hoqu x] pr. εν   AFM rell

The group is free from omissions according to M.T.

vii. 7 ὁ ἀδελφὸς αὐτοῦ BAM (mg) ir o qu Cyr] om. FM (txt) rell 𝔄𝔅ℭ𝔖
xi. 9 πληθύνων   B fir o q sc₂] om. AM rell 𝔄𝔅ℭ𝔏ᵛ𝔓𝔖
xvi. 26 ὅτι   B fir o q sb] om. AFM (txt) rell 𝔄𝔅ℭ𝔏ᵛ𝔖 Cyr
xviii. 4 λέγων   B fir o qu bk] om. AFM rell 𝔅ℭᶠ𝔏𝔖
xxiv. 15 καὶ ιησους   B fir o unx] om. AFM rell 𝔄ℭℭᶠ𝔏ᵛ𝔖 Eus
xxxv. 21 ἀφαίρεμα καὶ   B a firho qu mx] om. AFM rell 𝔄𝔅ℭ𝔏ʳʷ𝔖

The group differs from the M.T. in word order

iv. 19 σου / τὴν ψυχήν   BA a fir o qu n] tr. FM rell 𝔄𝔏ʳ Cyr
iv. 24 αὐτὸν ἀποκτεῖναι   BA a fir o qu s] tr. FM rell 𝔄 Cyr ⅓
vii. 2 σοὶ ἐντέλλομαι   BA fir o qu bwsn] tr. FM rell 𝔄𝔖 Cyr
vii. 6 αὐτοῖς κύριος   BA firho qu bwsn] tr. FM rell 𝔖
ix. 1 μοι λατρεύσωσιν   B fir o qu bw n] tr. AM rell 𝔄𝔅𝔓𝔖
xxxii. 28 ἐκείνη / τῇ ἡμέρᾳ   B a o qu nx 𝔏ʳʷᶻ Phil Luc] tr. AFM rell 𝔄 (uid) 𝔖
xxxiii. 20 μου / τὸ πρόσωπον   B rho u n] tr. AFM rell 𝔄𝔏ʳʷ Eus T–A

The group has a less literal translation

iv. 27 κατεφίλησαν ἀλλήλους   BA a fir o qu b s] κατεφιλησεν αυτον FM rell 𝔄𝔅ℭ𝔖
v. 8 ἀφελεῖς   BA a fir o qu a₂] αφελειτε FM rell 𝔄𝔅ℭ𝔏ʳ𝔖
vi. 27 καὶ ἐξήγαγον   BAa* (-γειν) ir o qu a₂sdn] ωστε εξαγαγειν FM rell 𝔄𝔅¹ℭ𝔖
xii. 45 ἤ   BM (mg) ir o qu s] και AFM (txt) rell 𝔄𝔅ℭ𝔖 Cyr
xii. 48 ποιῆσαι¹⁰   B fir o q sℭᶜ (uid) 𝔏ᶻ] και ποιη vel sim. AFM rell 𝔄𝔅ℭᶠ𝔖 Or-gr Or-lat
xvii. 2 λέγοντες B fir o qu bwkmn 𝔏ᶻ] και ελεγον AFM rell 𝔅𝔖 (txt) Eus
xviii. 5 ἐξῆλθεν B fir o qu] ηλθεν AFM rell 𝔄𝔅 (uid) ℭ𝔏ᶻ𝔖 Cyr Thdt

(For some parts of Exod. q is not extant: h joins the group very frequently in the last ten chapters.)

Here then is very clear evidence that B(A) afir oqu(xh) often witness to a text that has not been revised according to the M.T. There are many places, of course, where their text is not original but contains some mistake or other; and sometimes the other MSS. will have retained the original reading or will have had it restored by adaptation to the M.T. We have, for instance, already had occasion to reject a reading of Bahnr in xxxviii. 20 (see p. 48) and another reading of Bahqru in the same verse (see p. 40); for both readings made obvious nonsense. To these may be added another example from vii. 15. Here an original στήσῃ συναντῶν αὐτῷ has been corrupted as follows:

στηση συν αυτω   1m 𝔅¹
εση συναντων αυτω   BM iroqusb₂
εση συν αυτω   f

Again B itself is in Exodus, as in other books, full of individual mistakes, particularly omissions, through scribal carelessness. It shows, too, in places (for example xx. 19, 20) an extraordinary alternation in its spelling of the name Moses; sometimes having Μωυσης and sometimes Μωσης, which more nearly transliterates the Hebrew. Whether this results from the same carelessness or comes from revision according to the M.T., it often brings B into the company of the revised texts which naturally have the spelling which is nearer the Hebrew. B then, by itself, is a very faulty witness.

Likewise the prominent sub-groups fir and qu(x) by themselves present a very mixed text. It is interesting that in Genesis they both (fir particularly) have notable agreements with the early papyri 962, 911 and 961,[1] for it shows that they contain quite an early element (though early does not necessarily mean good). At the same time they have clearly suffered the results of cross-checking with later text types as is shown by their occasional doublets. In xxvii. 11, for example, BM(mg) hin Cyr. have πρὸς ἀπηλιώτην; AFM, the majority of the minuscules and the versions have πρὸς βορρᾶν. fiᵃˀr have a combination of the two, πρὸς βορρᾶν πρὸς ἀπηλιώτην.

The special readings of qux in Exodus are rarely of any value. The majority readings, for example in the two parallel passages xxiii. 18 and xxxiv. 25, are κοιμηθῇ and κοιμηθήσεται;

[1] Cf. H. A. Sander's account in his edition of the Berlin Genesis, Univ. of Michigan Studies: Human. Series, vol. XXI, pp. 256 ff.

μείνῃ is read by qux in xxiii. 18 and by F^b in xxxiv. 25 (q is not there extant), which makes it look as if F^b and qux were dependent on a common source. Again F^b qux are the main witnesses to the reading τὰ θηρία τοῦ ἀγροῦ in xxiii. 11 against the majority reading τὰ ἄγρια θηρία. Now F^b is a veritable miscellany of late readings, and in the closing chapters is a chief supporter of Origen's text. The agreement of qux with F^b, therefore, provides us with a clue to the source of much that is peculiar to qux.

When therefore we come to the closing chapters of the book we may expect that Bafirhoqux will have preserved some original readings against the revised readings of the other MSS. On the other hand these chapters, with their frequent repetition of technical terms and phrases, have given the freest rein to B's characteristic weakness of carelessness, so that the readings of AFM, etc., though agreeing more closely with the M.T., may not always be secondary on that account. Here, too, where editors have had much scope for revision, the sub-groups fir and qux may well contain much that is late. Thus in xxxix. 4 ἑκατόν^{2°} read by Bahqru and ἑκατόν^{3°} read by B alone are manifestly careless additions; their absence from the other MSS. is original although it means that these MSS. are here closer to the M.T. In xxxvii. 13 the ἑκατὸν πεντήκοντα of Bah is evidently wrong and the πέντε καὶ δέκα of the other MSS. correct.

But in ch. xxxviii there are many instances where the shorter readings seem original and the longer ones the result of revision. The whole passage is evidently intended to be a very abbreviated account of the furniture, so that the longer readings are immediately suspect. Moreover these longer readings are regularly found in the same group, AFM and their allies, and they consistently agree with the M.T. I quote a few examples:

xxxviii. 2 + καὶ ἐποίησεν αὐτῇ κυμάτιον χρυσοῦν κύκλῳ = M.T.
xxxviii. 3 + ἐπὶ τὰ τέσσαρα μέρη αὐτῆς = M.T.
xxxviii. 5 + καθαροῦ = M.T.
xxxviii. 6 καὶ τοὺς δύο] καὶ ἐποίησεν δύο = M.T.

We conclude therefore that the shorter text of these verses is likely to be original and that AFM, etc. have here a revised text, just as they so often have elswhere.

4. ORIGEN'S RELATION TO THE A-GROUP

The revision, however, is only very partial; it is far from being a complete revision like Origen's. It is interesting and profitable to study some of their differences. In its account of the making of the ark the M.T. gives a full description of the staves. In the Greek we should expect the corresponding account in xxxviii. 4, but in the LXX text there is only a passing mention of them in *v.* 4 and another slight mention of them in *v.* 11 in connection with the making of the staves for the table. In Origen's text there is, of course, an addition in the appropriate place to represent fully the M.T.'s account, but there is nothing of this addition in AFM, etc. Similarly in xxxvii. 8 Babx𝕴ʳ give merely the number of the court pillars and bases. AM and the majority, including the Origenic MSS., add the material, χαλκαῖ, and this agrees with the M.T.; but in the M.T. there is also another complete phrase—'the hooks of the pillars and their fillets of silver'—and only the Origenic MSS. have anything to represent this. And, in addition to small differences like these, there are the two outstanding facts that the text of AFM, etc. has not been changed to agree with the order of the M.T., as has Origen's text, and there has been no attempt to supply the big omissions (such as the making of the frames), as Origen has done.

We naturally ask whether this revision was made before or after Origen. It is not confined to Exodus; strong evidence of it is found throughout the Pentateuch and there is every reason to believe that it is pre-Origenic.[1] But in the closing chapters of Exodus Origen supplies some unexpected evidence that may suitably be discussed here. There are passages in these chapters so far removed from the M.T. that Origen does not attempt to correct them. Instead he first gives the LXX account under an obelus and then his own version. Now in the passages that he has revised, Origen will have followed his normal procedure:[2] he will have consulted several LXX MSS., chosen from them

[1] I have dealt slightly with the question in my unpublished Cambridge Ph.D. thesis 1954, and in the Tyndale Lecture for 1954 (London, 1955). I hope to deal with it fully in the near future in a detailed textual study of the whole of the Pentateuch. See p. 1 n., above.

[2] For a description of his procedure see Field, *Orig. Hex.* I, p. lx, IV. 1.

the readings nearest the M.T., and then added his own corrections. But in the passages that he has not attempted to correct, but has merely included *sub obelo*, he will presumably have followed the text of the first MS. that came to hand. We are thus able to compare the relation of Origen to the B and A texts in the corrected passages with his relation to them in the uncorrected. The main uncorrected passages are xxxviii. 9b–11, 13b–17, and 22. They are too short for over-wide generalizations to be made from their evidence, but it does appear that Origen favours neither type of text; where the MSS. are fairly widely and characteristically divided, Origen agrees almost as often with the one text type as with the other. And it should be repeated that the agreement is fortuitous; it does not proceed from Origen's estimation of the quality of the readings concerned, since he considered that these passages were too remote from the M.T. to be capable of revision. It means that in these passages Origen's 'random' *Vorlage* contained elements of both the B and A texts. The following list of examples is not exhaustive, but it gives the more widely disputed variants (Orig. = majority of Origenic MSS.):

xxxviii. 10 δακτυλίους B a b₂] + χρυσους AFM rell Orig 𝕭 𝕮ᶠ 𝕷ʳᶻ
xxxviii. 10 δύο¹ᵒ Bah fir no egsvz a₂b₂ Orig: + μεν bwx] + δακτυλιους AFM rell 𝕭 𝕮ᶠ 𝕷ʳ
xxxviii. 10 δύο²ᵒ Bah fir no egsvz a₂b₂ bw x Orig] + δακτυλιους AFM rell 𝕭
xxxviii. 16 τῶν ἄκρων BM (txt) ah f r n Orig: το ακρον x] + αυτων AFM (mg) rell 𝕭 𝕷ʳ
xxxviii. 17 αὐτῶν Ba ir o 𝕭] αυτης AFM rell Orig 𝕷ʳ
xxxviii. 22 ἦσαν Bah no b dpt qux Orig] ην AFM rell Cyr

But in the corrected passages Origen agrees much more often with the A-group readings for the simple reason that here Origen did exercise deliberate choice and, of the variants in the MSS. he consulted, he preferred the readings that were nearer the M.T. Taking these as his base he would then add his own corrections. We have already considered four readings from ch. xxxviii (2, 3, 5, 6) in which AFM and their allies had additions according to the M.T. If we now consult Origen's text we find that he has all four additions in exactly the same wording but without any asterisk; which means that these additions were already to be found in some of the MSS. he consulted. In the same context the additions which are not to be found in AFM etc. are all marked with asterisks; and this incidentally shows that here at least we may rely on the transmission of Origen's signs.

Other interesting points are raised by Origen's signs in these chapters. In xxxvii. 25 he has supplied an account of the making of the incense altar which is missing from the other MSS. The opening phrase stands thus: οὗτος ἐποίησεν τὸ θυσιαστήριον τὸ χρυσοῦν ※ ἐκ ξύλων ἀσήπτων. The position of the asterisk is remarkable; if it is correct, it means that some pre-Origenic MSS. contained a reference to the making of the incense altar. As it happens we can check the accuracy of the position of his signs in other similar places in the same chapter:

xxxviii. 1 (xxxvii. 1)   καὶ ἐποίησεν Βεσελεηλ τὴν κιβωτὸν ※ θ΄ ἐκ ξύλων ἀσήπτων.

xxxviii. 9 (xxxvii. 10)   καὶ ἐποίησεν τὴν τράπεζαν ÷ τὴν προκειμένην. . . .

Here the signs are correctly placed, for the opening phrases are still to be found in non-hexaplaric MSS. It is quite possible, therefore, that Origen did find the phrase οὗτος ἐποίησεν τὸ θυσιαστήριον τὸ χρυσοῦν in some of his MSS. It is even possible that the phrase was original and dropped out accidentally from all MSS. except the Origenic, for none of the pre-hexaplarically corrected MSS. has it.

Again, it has been demonstrated (pp. 91–3) that the rearrangement of the text which resulted in the present order of the Greek left behind some debris that got mixed up in wrong places. This was especially true of the phrase πάντα τὰ ἐργαλεῖα τῆς σκηνῆς τοῦ μαρτυρίου (xxxix. 10). It was suggested that in the original Greek text these words stood in their proper place preceded by καὶ συνετελέσθη, thus translating exactly the M.T., 'Thus was finished all the work of the tabernacle of the tent of meeting'. Origen's text reads (xxxix. 32): καὶ συνετελέσθη πάντα τὰ ἐργαλεῖα τῆς σκηνῆς ※ α΄ σ΄ σκέπης ⟨ τοῦ μαρτυρίου. Once more, the absence of an asterisk from the beginning of this sentence (if it faithfully reproduces Origen's work) means that Origen actually found these words in some of the MSS. he consulted.

It thus appears that some of the corruption and omission that has affected all our extant MSS. may be late and post-Origenic —which is not surprising. Once the order of the text had been so drastically altered and edited, it would open the gate to much subsequent corruption.

There is one further point arising from Origen's text. Origen nowhere has the portion xxxviii. 18–20 which we have contended is a free composition and not founded on any Hebrew text. This is striking, but we cannot be certain that these verses were missing from Origen's *Vorlage*. Where there is some Hebrew behind a Greek passage, however poor a rendering the Greek is, Origen retains it *sub obelo*. But here there is no M.T. authority at all; it may be therefore that Origen deliberately omitted the passage altogether.

INDEX

אֲרָנִים, inconsistent translations of, 44–51, 62

Altar
  copper
    description of, 17–18
    making of, 52
    omission of, 92
  golden, of incense
    description of, 17–18
    omission of, 3, 66–9, 76, 113
  utensils
    mistaken translations of, 53–4, 60–2

Authorised Version, mistakes in, 18, 86 n.

Bases, 15, 26–7, 44–50, 62, 71, 92 n.

Capitals, see κεφαλίδες

וָוִים, varying translations of, 21–2, 43–4

Editing, examples of, 43–4, 47, 53, 57, 75, 94, 97–8, 100–1

Fillets
  meaning of term, 15
  translations of, 26–7, 37–8
Finn, A. H., ix, 5 n., 38 n., 47 n., 64 n., 65 n., 67, 81, 101
Frames
  description of, 15
  omission of, 70, 74–5, 76

Gate-screen
  description of, 15
  mistake in measurements for, 25
  omission of, 70
Goats'-hair curtains
  confused translation of, 70, 73–4
  description of, 16
  omission of, 70, 72–3, 76
  technical term for, 16–17
Grate or Grating, 35, 53, 54, 72 n., 92

Katz, Peter, 1 n., 34 n., 35 n., 57 n., 61 n.
κεφαλίδες, strange usage of term, 21–3, 43, 44–51, 62

Lampstand
  description of, 18
  translation of terms relating to, 33–5, 55–7, 62–3
Laver
  description of, 18, 57
  omission of, 57–9, 69–72, 76
Lists
  confusion of, 65, 68, 71–2
  Greek fondness for, 81–2, 92 n.
  rearrangement of, 94–8
  unsatisfactoriness of, 49–51

McNeile, A. H., 5, 23 n., 32 f., 41, 43, 52, 57, 67 n., 84
Mercy-seat
  omission of, 58, 72
  translation of, 32, 34
Mistakes in translation, 20, 22, 25, 26, 27–8, 41–4, 45, 53, 60–2, 73, 84, 86 n., 95–6

Origins of Septuagint, 12–13

Pillars
  description of, 14–15
  frames confused with, 41–2
Points of the compass, 23–4
Popper, Julius, 5–6, 24, 30, 38–9, 75–6, 82–5, 89–91
Pre-Origenic revision, 1, 111–13

Revised Version, mistakes in, 16, 84

στολαί, true meaning of, 73, 89–91, 95, 97
στῦλοι
  double use of term, 20, 41–2
  mistaken identity, 41–2
  omission of, 74–5
σύνταξις, meaning of, 82–5
Swete, H. B., 4, 8 n., 11, 29, 30, 101

Tabernacle, strict technical meaning, 16–17
Targumic additions, 3, 6, 20, 55–6, 76
Tent, strict technical meaning, 16–17

Veil
  description of, 15
  varying translations of, 23, 37, 95–8
Vestments, significance of their position, 5, 31, 85–94